MW01101890

THE CAREER RESOURCE LIBRARY

Careers
in
Urban
Planning

Gillian Houghton

The Rosen Publishing Group, Inc.
NEW YORK

For Jason

Published in 2003 by The Rosen Publishing Group, Inc.
29 East 21st Street, New York, NY 10010

Copyright © 2003 by The Rosen Publishing Group, Inc.

First Edition

Cover © Yang Liu/ Corbis

Library of Congress Cataloging-in-Publication Data

Houghton, Gillian.
Careers in urban planning / Gillian Houghton.– 1st ed.
    p. cm. — (The career resource library)
Includes bibliographical references and index.
ISBN 0-8239-3658-9 (lib. bdg.)
1. City planning—Vocational guidance—United States.
I. Title. II. Series.
HT167 .H677 2003
307.1'216'02373—dc21

2002004889

Manufactured in the United States of America

Contents

So You Want to Be an Urban Planner?

1

Imagine having the power to alter not only the appearance but also the character of a city. Imagine having the ability not only to construct magisterial buildings, design beautiful urban parks, and install state-of-the-art transportation systems, but also to wage war against poverty and crime. Imagine having the potential to improve the lives of thousands of urban residents and help guarantee a safer, healthier, more prosperous city for generations to come. This is the power of urban planning.

What Is Urban Planning?

Urban planners develop land use plans to provide for the growth and revitalization of urban communities, while helping local officials make decisions concerning the social, economic, and environmental problems associated with those communities.

The main task of a planner is to promote the best use of a community's land and resources for a wide range of purposes—residential, commercial, municipal, and recreational. In carrying out this task, urban planners address issues such as snarled traffic, water quality, and the effects of growth and change on a community. They may formulate plans relating to the construction of community centers, affordable housing, or infrastructure (public works such as highways, roads, bridges, tunnels, and subway systems). Some planners are involved in environmental issues ranging from lead paint removal efforts to soil contamination programs, from open space preservation to the location of new landfills (large garbage dumps) or garbage incinerators. Because community development affects every member of a given community and is meant to improve the quality of life, planners often find themselves operating in the political sphere as well. For example, an urban planner may be called upon to help draft legislation on environmental, social, and economic issues, such as providing for low-income housing, developing water use regulations for periods of drought, or creating tax incentives for small-business owners.

A successful career in urban planning requires far more than an interest in building things. It must also include a strong commitment to people and their communities and a strong interest in economics, the law, and demographics (the statistical study of a given population or group of people). Good urban planners examine proposed community facilities, such as schools, jails, and airports, to be sure that these facilities will meet the changing demands placed upon them over time and serve the community well. They study the latest economic and legal issues involved in zoning codes, building codes, and environmental regulations. They ensure that builders and developers follow these codes and regulations and do not take advantage of or endanger community residents. Planners also deal with land use issues created by the increasing suburbanization of North America.

Before preparing plans for a proposed development on a certain piece of land, planners report on how that land is currently being used, its shortcomings, and how its potential can be better tapped to create a more thriving and pleasant community. These reports include information on the location and capacity of streets, highways, water and sewer lines, schools, libraries, and cultural and recreational sites. They also provide data on the types of industries in the surrounding area, a profile of its residents, and employment and economic trends. With this information, planners design the layout of the proposed facilities and prepare reports showing how their projects can be carried out, what they will cost, and how they will benefit the community and its residents.

How a Planner Sees Things

Take a walk down a busy street in a town or city near you. How tall are the buildings that surround you? What percentage of them are homes? Businesses? Factories or industrial plants? Are the buildings well maintained and attractive? How wide is the street? Does traffic flow smoothly? Is the sidewalk lined with trees, benches, bus stops, newsstands, lampposts, and wastebaskets? Do billboards and on-site business advertisements obstruct the view? Are the air and water clean? Is the surrounding land good for farming? Are people gathered in public spaces? How do they relate to one another? Do the people who live nearby have access to public transportation?

Next, visit a local park or playground, a public promenade, a civic center, a library, a museum, or a center of commerce. Are there people taking advantage of these spaces? Who are they and why are they there? How do their daily schedules relate to how and when they enjoy the space? How does their presence affect others in the space?

These are just some of the many questions posed by an urban planner as he or she considers the communities in which we live. Collaborating with a team of planning professionals that includes surveyors, engineers, environmentalists, lawyers, and social action workers, urban planners work to make the lives of all community residents, especially those in underdeveloped or poor neighborhoods, better.

The word "better," however, is often a matter of opinion at best and, at worst, highly controversial. Where one resident sees change as a new opportunity for a neighborhood, another may see it as a threat to an established way of life. So an urban planner must be a skilled diplomat, putting together compromises between various individuals and interest groups that have differing notions of what "better" means. An urban planner must be aware of these controversies, as well as legal precedents, budget limitations, and economic trends. Many urban planners argue that every act of government—from increasing the defense budget to amending welfare programs and supporting education reform, for example—is an indirect act of urban planning. All government policies affect where and how people live, what jobs are available to them, and how they view their communities. The work of urban planning, therefore, requires a working knowledge of and skill in several very different disciplines—architecture, engineering, social policy, politics, law, and economics.

This book will introduce you to the work of professional urban planners and provide glimpses into the related tasks performed by other members of the urban planning community, including professional designers, researchers, activists, community developers, politicians, council members, lawyers, accountants, and businesspeople. It will also provide you with valuable information about educational requirements, urban planning programs, internships, and strategies for getting your first job in planning. As you consider any career path, it is important to assess your strengths and explore the many areas of specialization—in the case of urban planning, this ranges from organizing petitions to drawing up architectural blueprints—to find one that fits your personality and skills.

Planning at a Glance

•A planner develops projects and policies to meet the social, economic, and physical needs of communities. He or she also develops the strategies necessary to put these plans into action.

•A planner considers the whole community when developing projects, including issues of housing, parks

and recreation, highways and transportation, environmental protection, and economic development.

•A planner must be both technically skilled and
creative. He or she must have the ability to imagine
improved alternatives to the communities we live in and
have the ability to turn that vision into reality.

•A planner must act as a mediator between competing community interests and viewpoints and devise the
best solutions to these conflicts.

•A planner educates public officials, interest groups,
and private citizens about the problems, alternatives,
and implications of a certain project. This allows them
to make knowledgeable, responsible choices.

A Brief History of the American City

2

Modern communities are a complicated web of local, state, and federal government regulations, private and nonprofit corporations, advocacy groups (organizations that represent a certain group of people or a certain viewpoint), and individual needs and desires. In large part, changes to urban environments are made by organizations. These include planning associations and private firms that successfully navigate their way through a complex bureaucratic maze of local zoning boards, state and federal grant applications, the petitions of community activists, and the pressures of private business interests. These and many other public and private sector hurdles must be cleared before new development projects and building plans can proceed.

Communities, however, can also grow and evolve independently of these organized efforts. Positive neighborhood change and development is often the result of the grassroots campaigning of ordinary residents. The persistent demands, creative solutions, and intimate knowledge offered by a community's residents can allow for the renewal of a neighborhood from "the bottom up" rather than being a plan imposed upon citizens by a bureaucracy, politician, or development corporation.

Unfortunately, just as communities can be renewed, they can also wither and die if they are poorly planned or neglected. Underlying racial and socioeconomic prejudices, the growth of the national highway system, and advancements in technology are just some of the social and cultural factors that affect the way we live, work, and play and whether our neighborhoods thrive or wither. Often, communities deteriorate, are abandoned, or become crime-ridden in the absence of—and in spite of—organized plans. This has been a characteristic of towns and cities in America since the founding of the first colonial settlements.

The History of Movement

In colonial America, communities were small and isolated. Throughout the eighteenth century, thanks to advancements in farming equipment and technique, the populations of rural areas (where economic opportunity was greatest) grew faster than those of towns and cities. In 1690, only a tenth of the colonial population lived in areas considered urban by seventeenth century standards. These urban centers were primarily maritime trade outposts that served as transit points for goods coming into the colonies or being sent out to the mother countries (such as England, France, the Netherlands, and Spain). By 1790, seven years after the end of the American Revolution, urban residents in the former colonies made up only 5 percent of the total population, indicating that more and more Americans tried to make their fortune from the land.

Independence from Britain, however, helped usher in a period of important social, political, and demographic changes that eventually resulted in the sudden and rapid growth of many American cities. Large increases in urban populations were spurred by innovations in manufacturing facilities (which brought new jobs to the cities), by the growing network of ships, railroads, canals, and national roads that carried goods from place to place (which made cities important links in a national chain of commerce), and by waves of immigrants from Europe (who found work and housing more easily in urban centers).

This rapid growth of cities may also be the result of what is often described as the uniquely American characteristic of restless exploration and expansion: manifest destiny. Many planning theorists have attributed much of the history of urban development to America's desire to pioneer and cultivate the land that lay beyond "civilization." Many of the demographic and geographic changes discussed later in this chapter, among them suburbanization, have been explained as the result, in part, of manifest destiny.

Growing Pains

By 1830, urban populations were on the rise, again climbing to 10 percent of the national population for the first time since 1690 and steadily increasing. Major urban centers, such as Boston, Philadelphia, New York, and Chicago, grew by leaps and bounds. For example, in 1820, New York had a population of 137,000. By 1870, that figure had reached 1.5 million, and more than 5 million people resided in New York by 1920.

As industrialized cities grew in size and population, they also developed a more complicated hierarchy of political organizations (such as political parties and trade unions), private interests (like industrialists), and class systems. The often competing needs and desires of each of these many groups helped influence the way cities were built and organized.

In addition, cities came to be geographically organized according to certain patterns of land use. In early industrial centers, for example, squares, churches, and administrative buildings at the city's core were flanked by wealthy residential areas. Suburbs—originally rickety tenements that were home to the middle and lower classes—surrounded these first modern cities, well away from the city's wealthy and centrally-located neighborhoods. While the rich lived close to shops, places of entertainment, and important seats of power and influence, the poor were situated within walking distance of their jobs at the outlying factories. They remained cut off from much that the city had to offer wealthier residents.

As industries continued to expand, city centers—crowded and dirtied by the increasing number of commercial and manufacturing ventures—became undesirable as upper-middle and upper class residential areas. The wealthy moved out to the surrounding countryside beyond the working class suburbs, newly accessible by horse-drawn buses, streetcars, and, by the 1860s, the electric trolley. The former single-family townhouses of the wealthy were left vacant, bought by slumlords, and rented out to several low-income families at a time. Due to the landlords' negligence and greed, these once grand buildings began to deteriorate, serving as an early example of what is now called inner-city blight.

The Rise of the Suburbs

Transportation would prove to be one of the most significant forces affecting the development of American cities. Suburbs, havens for the upper classes escaping the grit and grime of creeping industrialization, were developed along streetcar and commuter train lines. In the early history of public transportation, fares charged for rides on streetcars and trains were unaffordable for most members of the working class. This further reinforced the growing divide between the urban poor and the suburban rich.

A variety of factors contributed to the success of suburban communities. Following the Great Depression and World War II, the government began offering low federal mortgage rates, which encouraged the middle class to buy homes by making them more affordable. At the same time, the government also gave homeowners new tax breaks and subsidized construction projects. Elaborate highway systems—generally a large loop ringing the city with spokes extending from the city center to the outer limits of the suburbs—were built to connect suburbanites with the business and cultural centers of the city, bringing them back in to the offices, shops, restaurants, and theaters of downtown. In addition, highways were intended to redistribute traffic and combat roadway congestion as a growing number of automobiles crowded the narrow city streets, which were originally built for horse-drawn buggies.

The plan backfired, however. Rather than bringing suburbanites into the city to work and spend money, the highway systems made it easier for former city dwellers to leave the city behind forever. With the establishment of highways came jobs, shops, and houses. More and more farmland was developed and paved over to make room for subdivisions, shopping centers, and office complexes. Soon, there was no reason to make the long journey into the city and its dirty, crime-ridden streets. The good life was to be found in the suburbs, where families could work, shop, go to school, and play in clean, safe neighborhoods.

Soon these suburban areas grew apart from the cities that had spawned them. Business and industry, lured by plenty of inexpensive land, had followed the droves of city dwellers that had moved to the suburbs in search of peace and quiet. The first shopping malls were built in the 1920s, and shoppers flocked to the suburban outposts of downtown stores, such as Sears, Hudson's, and Marshall Field's. In fact, many of the downtown flagship branches of these department stores eventually closed after losing customers to their suburban sister stores.

The relocation of businesses became a driving force in the organization of suburban communities. Suburbs became independent, self-governed townships with community standards and values that began to diverge from those of city dwellers. Where the cities were multicultural and allowed for various kinds of lifestyles, many suburban communities encouraged conformity and racial segregation. To make sure that the new, independent town centers of the suburbs maintained their distinct moral, ethnic, and philosophical homogeneity (or sameness), local governments armed themselves with a powerful weapon: zoning ordinances.

The Evolution of Zoning

At the beginning of America's colonial history, rural land was regulated to ensure that British merchants would have access to cheap goods. There were few other restrictions; the colonial outposts were essentially self-governed. Residents often came together for the purpose of mutual aid and protection, but there were no conscious efforts to maintain the character of the neighborhood.

In an attempt to create utopian societies (perfect communities), several early American cities—among them Savannah, Georgia, and Philadelphia, Pennsylvania—were precisely laid out with central and outlying parks and streets mapped out on a grid. Cities, such as Manhattan, that were established for the pursuit of economic rather than religious fulfillment, grew up more spontaneously. As such, they were often a cramped and disorganized mix of homes and industries. Extremes of wealth and poverty existed side-by-side, often sparking social strife. The crowded conditions and industrial pollution led to widespread sickness. Extreme poverty resulted in high crime rates. In an attempt to impose order upon this chaos, city government intervened. The first city ordinances were primarily intended to promote the general health and safety of the city's residents and to combat the new evils of industrialized city life.

In most early American urban centers—before and after colonial independence—commerce was the driving force. Local governments did not try to interfere with the pursuit of wealth by instituting wide-ranging public controls over land use and planning. People were largely free to do what they wanted with the land they owned. Following American independence, however, city and state governments became more powerful as a multitude of private economic pursuits, such as large-scale transportation systems, required cooperation between government and private enterprise. One of the most famous examples of this public-private partnership was the creation of the Erie Canal, which connected the port of Manhattan to Lake Ontario through the Hudson River and a series of human-made waterways.

This feat of engineering, completed in 1825, was the work of powerful New York State businesspeople, who wanted to open new markets in the country's interior for their goods, and enthusiastic politicians, who were drawn to the jobs created by the project and the tax dollars generated by the new commerce and development along the canal. Over time, government became the puppet of private business interests, ushering in a period of laissez-faire rule (French for "free to do") in which the government allowed industry to operate with very few restrictions or regulations. It was thought that getting in the way of private enterprise would only drag the American economy down, leading to even more social problems. Generating wealth would do more to solve society's ills than government intrusion ever could, according to this theory. It didn't hurt that politicians were often rewarded for their hands-off attitude to business, in the form of bribes. A new era of American urban politics—led by such famously corrupt politicians as New York's Boss Tweed and the men of Tammany Hall—was born. The result was that politicians and industrialists got richer, while unprotected workers were exploited and sank deeper into poverty and desperation. As a result, American cities became even more sharply divided, violent, and disease-ridden.

City Beautiful

By the late 1880s, political reformers stood up in protest, ushering in the first of America's nationwide urban renewal plans, the City Beautiful movement, which sought to create a livable city that was more clean, ordered, and comfortable for all of its residents. This was an era of monumental buildings, wide boulevards, forest preserves, and housing codes that regulated dense residential areas, such as tenements (an indirect attempt to control a supposedly unruly working class). These projects were designed to rejuvenate urban areas and preserve the country's natural resources. For example, New York's Central Park was created as an oasis of well-groomed nature in the center of a bustling city, to be enjoyed by the wealthy and the working poor alike. Today, however, the City Beautiful movement is often criticized because it effectively isolated cultural and civic centers in large and imposing monuments that were less than inviting to members of the lower classes. While these constructions were undeniably beautiful and impressive, they were also quite intimidating. As a result, these buildings often failed to become popular meeting places, and the surrounding areas suffered from neglect.

Garden City

Another new movement in planning that gained increasing popularity at the close of the nineteenth century was the dream of the Garden City. When addressing the problems of urban residential areas, theorists turned to Englishman Ebenezer Howard. Howard's Garden City philosophy envisioned idyllic suburban communities—retreats from the social ills of the city—where the houses were turned away from the curving street to face a circular expanse of communal land. Many modern-day subdivisions attempt, in part, to re-create Howard's vision of a more pastoral community. The Garden City philosophy, however, also led to suburban sprawl—the massive, decentralized waves of housing developments that spread ever farther outward from the city and drained urban areas of a middle class, the jobs and shops that went with them, and a valuable tax base.

Howard's theories would also eventually be applied to the subsidized, high-rise urban housing projects of the mid-twentieth century, with devastating results. Whereas a sense of distance from thoroughfares is valuable in the suburbs, in the cities it creates secluded areas that become staging areas for crime. The high-rise public housing tower that sits on an isolated "campus" with several similar towers has been widely discredited in recent years and blamed for providing an ideal breeding ground for violent crime, drug use, and drug dealing because of its many dark corridors and stairwells and its inaccessibility to the street.

The Collaboration of Zoning and Planning

Despite its shortcomings, the late nineteenth and early twentieth centuries were a fruitful period in American planning history that resulted in a greater commitment to the study of planning, environmental protection, and historic preservation. The New York State Tenement House Law was enacted in 1901. The first formal study of urban design was begun by students in Harvard College's Landscape Architecture Department in 1909. The National Park Service was created in 1916 with the mission of preserving the nation's natural, historical, and cultural resources. In 1921, the city government of New Orleans, Louisiana, formed the Vieux Carre Commission, the first organization of its kind, to work to preserve New Orleans's historic landmarks.

Throughout the first two decades of the twentieth century, towns and cities across America experimented with the best way to create efficient, planned communities. Social theorists and community developers tried to make planning a new kind of science, though one with few proven principles. Planners began to study the inner-workings of their cities in an attempt to figure out how so many separate and distinct elements fit together and what complex web of influences determines whether a city, a neighborhood, or a single block will succeed or become the next Skid Row.

The American Planning Association (APA) at Work: The Growing Smart Project

The Growing Smart Project is an effort by the APA to draft the next generation of planning and zoning legislation. To this end, the APA has published the Growing Smart Legislative Guidebook, which details the tools available to state and local governments to help fight urban sprawl, protect rapidly disappearing farmland, promote affordable housing, and encourage redevelopment of depressed areas.

When these efforts were met with what seemed to be insurmountable complications—exceptions to every proposed rule or principle were discovered—planning turned toward land use regulations and zoning, elements of urban planning that were precise and controlled. Through zoning—classifying areas as residential, commercial, industrial, recreational, and so forth—immediate progress could be made toward determining the character and activity of a given neighborhood.

Zoning, however, is not the same thing as planning. It is concerned only with how the land can and will be used within the legal framework of a community. It does nothing to develop that land or solve the tough questions associated with development, such as how to create a pleasant neighborhood that can comfortably accommodate residents and workers, homes and businesses, pedestrians and cars. Cities, states, and the federal government have the authority to determine how certain areas will be used in the best interests of a community's health and welfare, and, as such, zoning decisions require little public input. Zoning primarily serves to prevent unwanted construction, such as large manufacturing plants built in residential areas or a string of bars and nightclubs in family-oriented neighborhoods.

In 1922, Congress passed the Standard State Zoning Enabling Act (SSZEA), which provided a model for zoning that could be adopted by each state as it saw fit. The act required that zoning be used as a tool to lessen traffic congestion, protect buildings from fire, raise the standards of public health and welfare, provide light and fresh air to apartment dwellers, and avoid creating areas of high population density. It would also provide communities with public transportation, utilities, schools, and other public works. In the coming years, hundreds of local city governments would follow the lead of state legislators in implementing complex zoning codes, changing the nature of urban planning in America significantly.

While the seemingly civic-minded aims of SSZEA established the basis of zoning law in America, other less noble goals of community zoning ordinances soon became evident. Zoning quickly became a tool to maintain middle-class (and often white) homeowner's property values by excluding potential homeowners on the basis of socioeconomic criteria. For example, zoning allows communities to regulate the minimum interior dimensions of a single family home, the minimum acreage of land required for that single family home, the number of acceptable units in an apartment building, and the presence of mobile homes.

These controls often serve to maintain the ethnic, social, and geographic homogeneity of an area by excluding those people—generally large, extended minority or immigrant families escaping the city just as the established suburbanites' parents did—who cannot afford to buy housing that meets these standards. The established residents and acceptable new arrivals (who fit the desired racial, ethnic, and socioeconomic mold) attempt to maintain the "character" of a neighborhood or residential development, at least until they move on to bigger, better, or more remote homes, finally making room for the groups of people they tried so hard to exclude earlier. This "trickle-down" method of home ownership provides an inadequate supply of affordable housing, however, so the development of government subsidized low-income housing units becomes necessary.

Careers in Urban Planning

This is the American cityscape at the beginning of the twenty-first century. In general, the wealthiest members of a community live in pastoral subdivisions and gated communities (the gate serving as an even more concrete barrier to the unwanted "city" element) far from the city center, while the poorest people live in deteriorating suburban homes in the neighborhoods closest to the city, and in poorly-conceived, often dangerous housing projects within the city limits.

American urban planning in the twentieth century was marked by a dependence on zoning, which is itself the result of our unique American history. Today's urban planner, however, is faced with a dense tangle of social, cultural, and political issues when considering a project. These include the environment, economic development and empowerment, community development, and transportation. Planning has shifted from the philosophy of urban renewal and the Model Cities Program of the 1960s to the philosophy of conservation and "empowerment zones" (both of which will be discussed in more depth in the following chapter). Today's urban planners must study the lessons of the past and, with a combination of daring creativity and time-tested methods, help build the cities of the future.

What Is an Urban Planner?

3

At the end of the twentieth century, there were about 30,000 urban planners employed in the United States, according to the American Planning Association (APA), a trade group of urban planning professionals. They work for private, public, and nonprofit organizations, but the majority—two out of three planners—were employed by state and local government agencies. They work for groups like San Francisco's Bay Area Rapid Transit District, the Austin (TX) Capitol Area Planning Council, and the Peoria County Planning and Zoning Department in Illinois, to name just a few of the thousands of nonprofit and government organizations operating across the country. An increasing number of planners, however, work in the private sector, for real estate developers, transportation companies, or private design firms. Planners work in towns and cities. They teach in universities and study urban problems firsthand. They advise government councils on urban policy decisions, lobby for legislation that affects urban development, and canvass neighborhoods door-to-door to learn about a community's needs and wants and to promote their proposed projects.

Because of this wide range of tasks, a group of planners might be hard-pressed to tell you what planning is. The scope of planning varies from city to city and from one agency to another. A planner in a larger or government-run organization might specialize in a very specific, narrowly focused type of planning project, such as those involving transportation, social services, or environmental issues. On the other hand, a planner in a small, private firm may work on a wide variety of projects, shifting with ease from one discipline or specialization to the next (such as sanitation, infrastructure, traffic flow, and the creation of public "green spaces"). This implies a great deal of freedom, but it is also one of planning's greatest challenges. The planner must look at each project and anticipate the many engineering, legal, political, cultural, and social issues it will raise. This is a daunting task indeed.

The Nature of the Job

We can, however, make some generalizations across the profession. The practicing planner usually approaches a project—whether it be to ease the traffic congestion that chokes a particular intersection, or to reclaim a city square that is plagued by crime, or to contain the suburban sprawl of an entire geographic region—by conducting geographic surveys and economic, social, and environmental tests. The planner might learn of residents' attitudes and desires by going door-to-door, approaching people in public spaces, or mailing surveys to a target group. He or she may interview community members, local business owners, and politicians to understand what they envision for a given neighborhood. The planner might study the patterns of human behavior and movement in an area over an extended period of time using personal observation or time-lapse photography in order to determine what sort of development would work best in this community. When all the data is collected, the planner must analyze and interpret their significance with respect to immediate, short-term, and long-term planning needs. This developmental phase of a project is undertaken in conjunction with economic analysts, lawyers, designers, and architects.

Next, the planner will create drawings, blueprints, models, or maps to outline his or her plans. Unfortunately, many of even the best conceived plans fail to be implemented for one reason or another (often having little to do with the project's strength and usefulness), and the resulting disappointment is in the very nature of urban planning. Successful planners, however, must move on to the next site or situation, investing each project with their full attention, energy, enthusiasm, and expertise.

Though some planners are self-employed and others work as freelance consultants (hired by companies to work on a specific project and free to work elsewhere upon its completion), most planners work in traditional office environments and spend at least forty hours per week at the office. While urban and regional planners spend much of their time working in an office, they are often also required to travel to inspect the plot of land under consideration for development or regulation, including its layout, natural features, current use, and existing structures. Some local government planners involved in site development inspections spend most of their time in the field. Planners may experience the pressure of deadlines and tight work schedules, as well as political pressure generated by interest groups affected by land use proposals.

In addition to their regular workday, planners frequently attend seminars, evening or weekend meetings with elected officials and government agencies, or public hearings with citizens' groups. Many planners are compelled by deadlines to do additional work at home and on the weekends. Planning projects are frequently deadline-driven, and successful planners are well-organized and responsible.

Job opportunities for urban planners continue to expand. Unprecedented economic growth throughout the 1990s, population increases as a result of higher birth rates and immigration, and a likely wave of retirements in the field all make it likely that residential and commercial building projects will continue to increase as will the demand for planners. State and local governments face the daunting task of providing housing and transportation for more and more residents while respecting the interests of a growing number of environmental and social action groups, historic preservation societies, and private business interests.

This expanding market presents numerous opportunities for young, idealistic planners. In order to find the particular planning specialization that best suits your interests and beliefs, you should become familiar with the most popular planning philosophies and strategies. While the following specializations are not entirely separate disciplines, this list will illustrate the basic distinctions between the different schools of thought and methods that are currently popular in modern urban planning. Furthermore, this list is not complete; it is only a selection of the most common areas of urban studies. An understanding of the history of these specializations is necessary in considering the larger trends in planning theory and, for the purposes of this book, in introducing you to the nature of planning policy.

Land Use Planning

Land use planning is the decision-making process that determines how a certain area of land will be developed and for what purposes. As discussed previously, the allocation and regulation of land has been central to American planning history. The restrictions placed by state governments on city zoning boards differ from state to state. In general, however, local authorities have adopted as their exclusive right the power to enact zoning ordinances with respect to location and use of land, as long as those ordinances do not intend to discriminate against a certain group of people or result in the intentional loss of land or income for a resident or business.

For much of zoning's history (as discussed in the previous chapter), this authority was used to protect the interests of private ownership, while ensuring the provision of public services for a community. More recently, modern land use planning has, in several cases, been used to curb the effects of decentralization advocated by the Garden City theorists of the 1920s. In the 1960s and 1970s, zoning became a powerful, if controversial, weapon in fighting suburban sprawl, the over-development of former farmland with strip malls and subdivisions. Several towns and cities attempted to institute phased growth plans whereby business and residential developments on the outer boundaries of a community were restricted in number or scope by city ordinance. The following examples are intended to illustrate the extent to which state and federal courts allowed local governments to control the rate of urban growth.

Ramapo, New York, is a large Long Island town about thirty miles from Manhattan. By the late 1960s, its population had reached 76,000, and local utilities, public services, and infrastructure were unable to meet the needs of a growing population. In response, the city enacted a comprehensive, eighteen-year planning program to curb the rate of residential development by requiring developers to apply for special building permits. If the site of development was within the service area of local utilities, the permit was granted. If the site was farther out and no local utilities had been built to that distance, then the developer was given the option of building the utilities himself or herself or waiting until they were extended to that point under the city's own program of expansion. Developers challenged the ordinance in court, and the court upheld the city's right to restrain growth in proportion to the city's existing financial resources. This was an important case because it allowed the city to enact zoning ordinances that were dependent not only on location and land use but also on the passage of time.

Another example, that of a growth management plan in Petaluma, California, illustrates the court's willingness to allow city zoning commissions to create exclusionary ordinances for the overall benefit of a community. It also demonstrates a relatively rare attempt to use zoning to achieve progressive social ends—in this case, affordable housing. By 1970, the once modest town of Petaluma had been annexed by the San Francisco–area housing market. San Francisco residents were leaving the city and seeking more affordable housing in more peaceful surroundings, while still being within commuting distance to the city. As a result, the population, which had been 10,000 in 1950, had soared to 25,000 in twenty years. The city imposed a residential development quota of 500 new dwellings each year, excluding developments of four units or less. The 500 permitted dwellings would be chosen from a pool of proposed designs judged on their proximity to utilities not yet overburdened by the growing community, on their inclusion of low-income units, on their use of open space, on their design, and on their creation of needed public works. The ordinance also provided that between 8 and 12 percent of the yearly quota would be met by low-cost units.

Local developers challenged the ordinance in court, citing its exclusionary nature (by forbidding certain sized subdivisions and the development of certain areas of town). The court, however, found that the ordinance was conceived for the common good, and it is within the city's right to make such determinations. In addition, the zoning ordinance was not exclusionary in the traditional sense of the word, in that it made special efforts to encourage low-cost housing. The zoning commission's rights were upheld.

These and similar land use cases constitute an extensive body of legal precedent regarding zoning law. Planners, especially those specializing in land use planning, must be familiar with this history to work within the legal framework of modern planning. As we will see in subsequent sections of this chapter, land use planning is used in conjunction with several other planning specialties when conceiving of and implementing a project.

Social and Community Development Planning

Social and community development planning attempts to involve those most directly affected by a proposed project—the area's residents—in the planning process, either by taking into account their needs and desires or by making them full and active partners in the work. It is an approach that became popular in the 1960s, as a response to the spiraling ills of American cities, including poverty and violence.

The early 1960s heralded the beginning of an era of great social turbulence and unrest following the placid and prosperous Eisenhower years of the 1950s. Crime rates rose dramatically, the civil rights movement moved to the center of the political and social stage, and urban poverty grew as a new wave of middle class residents began to flee the cities. In response, Americans became increasingly disenchanted with the urban renewal policies of the previous generation, exemplified by the construction of monolithic housing projects that were seen as dehumanizing and oppressive. The government, under presidents John F. Kennedy and Lyndon B. Johnson, enacted many varied legislative policies and programs as part of the war on poverty. They provided funds and services such as food stamps, job training, and health clinics. They also experimented with planning projects such as the Model Cities Program and the

Community Action Program. In addition, the Department of Housing and Urban Development (HUD) was created in 1965, the first federal agency focused exclusively on urban policy.

President Richard Nixon replaced this loose array of federal programs with the more flexible system of categorical block grants (money given to local governments for a certain general purpose, but to be spent at the local government's discretion), including the Community Development Block Grant (CDBG) program. The CDBG program allocated money to city governments for the purpose of creating decent, affordable housing and a livable environment. The money was never tracked, however, results were never monitored, and the programs never reviewed by HUD or any other federal agency. Consequently, federal funds were sometimes put toward questionable projects, including recreational facilities in affluent neighborhoods and snow removal operations that should have been paid for by the regular city budget. Planners differ on whether the CDBG program was effective over time, despite occasional abuses and misdirection of funds. Though it served as a powerful tool in addressing problems facing the urban poor, many argued that local governments too often allocated the program's resources to areas not in the greatest need and spread money too thinly. Nevertheless, in the 1990s, the program was enlarged by the Clinton administration, which allocated a $690 million increase over five years to create an estimated 60,000 new jobs.

In 1978, President Jimmy Carter proposed a "new partnership" to combat various urban problems, focusing on the cooperation of various federal and state agencies, the private sector, and the public at large, working as volunteer organizations and individuals. The attendant legislation, the Urban Development Action Grants (UDAG), was intended to encourage private investment in depressed areas by offering development grants.

The program was of limited success and indirectly required stricter government controls over urban aid projects. However, the legacy of Carter's "new partnership" survives today in the form of some 2,000 community development corporations (CDCs) across the country. The aims of the community development movement are to jump-start the economy of a community, to improve the physical appearance and organization of a community, and to forge social bonds among residents. These corporations make partnerships with a variety of local or national businesses and government agencies to provide goods and services to residents and sponsor long-term projects that will benefit the community for years.

CDCs are created and maintained by community residents, who are sometimes called "social entrepreneurs" because CDCs are finance-based organizations that operate like any other complicated business. Though not for profit, they must be run efficiently if they are to survive and continue raising funds. CDCs are not solely concerned with traditional social activism because, in addition to identifying and publicizing the problem, they also participate actively in the solution. CDCs are also not charity organizations or grant foundations because they work to provide goods, services, and livable environments, rather than simply oversee the allocation of money to other organizations who do the community-based work.

The work of CDCs in America is impressive, though it differs widely in scope and success from one organization to another. An estimated 30,000 units of affordable housing are built by CDCs each year. They build and operate health clinics, supermarkets, shopping malls, and nursing homes to provide basic community services to dozens of distressed neighborhoods each year. In 1997, CDCs invested $1.9 billion in 59,000 small, independent businesses. CDCs have created 247,000 jobs in private businesses and offered job training and career counseling to thousands of people. What began as a grassroots movement has become a national philosophy and a multimillion dollar business.

Community development is the product of many public and private agencies, ranging from tenant organizations and faith-based community groups to community development banks and state financing agencies. Planners play an important role within CDCs, addressing housing needs, studying successful crime prevention techniques, and beautifying public spaces. Their recommendations for community improvement often determine which projects are accepted and funded and how money is spent.

Economic Development Planning

Throughout its history, economic development planning—finding ways to promote sustained investment in a community—has been an aspect of community development, but it has recently taken on a new life of its own, in the form of enterprise (renamed empowerment) zones, or EZs, and enterprise communities, or ECs.

President Ronald Reagan's economic stimulus package, nicknamed the Reagan Revolution, was based primarily upon deregulation. Reagan believed that business and industry would flourish only when given the freedom to operate independently of government controls, oversight, and regulations. To that end, Reagan cut costly domestic aid programs, federal income taxes, and federally-funded social services, including the Urban Development Action Grant program. He argued that the private sector—corporations, charitable foundations, and individual donors—and not government could best look after the interests of struggling communities and their residents. Natural market forces, he claimed, would create a pattern of equal and livable urban settlement. In addition, the economy would be strong enough to overcome social problems such as crime, unemployment, and poverty. In fact, Reagan reasoned, government efforts to curb these social ills were not only ineffective; they actually contributed further to the problems of cities by misspending money and creating a "culture of dependence"—a community used to government handouts rather than enterprise and initiative.

The only proactive urban policy initiative propose by the Reagan administration was the enterprise zon Reagan nominated seventy-five urban areas to receive ti status of enterprise zones. The aim was to stabilize an improve the economies of these areas, with the active involvement of community organizations, by favoring the development of small, local businesses that would funnel profits back into the community (rather than to a corporate headquarters located out of state or even out of country). The government would encourage this process by providing tax breaks to start-up companies.

Though popular, Reagan's enterprise zone legislation was rejected by Congress during his term and that of his successor, George H. W. Bush. The program, renamed "empowerment zones" and broadened to include "enterprise communities," was finally approved in 1993, following the election of Bill Clinton. Today, 110 empowerment zones across the country receive $2.5 billion per year in tax breaks and block grants, in addition to substantial support from state and local agencies, academic institutions, and private businesses.

Equity Planning

Under the heading of economic development also comes equity planning. Many experts in the field argue that equity planning attacks the root of the economic disparity apparent in cities, rather than simply applying a series of bandages to the problem. As the name suggests, equity planners strive to create communities in which socially or economically disadvantaged people, such as the elderly, disabled, or poor, are given additional opportunities to level the economic playing field. These planners support proposals or policies that provide funds and resources to the disadvantaged, and they lobby against those programs that instead benefit the traditional recipient of political perks: the affluent.

For example, a group of equity planners might campaign against the construction of a high-end shopping center or a corporate office plaza supported by city funds and tax breaks. These projects generally benefit the developers, the owners, and a small group of affluent consumers and employees, few of whom actually live in the community. Conversely, equity planners might draft or support proposals that offer discounts on bus fares for certain disadvantaged members of the community, such as the elderly or disabled, who depend on public transportation. They might support programs that provide literacy training, free health services, employment counseling, affordable public utilities (such as gas and electricity), or job development courses for the disenfranchised. In many American cities, equity planning has become a successful tool for providing goods and services to those often overlooked in the development of urban areas. The thinking is that equity programs will create a healthier, more educated, and wealthier community population. As a result, their neighborhoods will also become safer and more vibrant.

Like all urban planners, equity planners must look at any given proposal from all angles. How will this project affect the target group (in this case, the disadvantaged) in financial terms? Will it provide short- or long-term employment? Will it improve their access to public transit, public health and education facilities, and the city's cultural life? In addition, equity planners must be careful negotiators and diplomatic political analysts. They must be adept at forming coalitions and making deals. When combating the forces of big business, development companies, politicians beholden to big money campaign contributors, and popular opinion, they put themselves squarely in the center of an often raging controversy.

Environmental Planning

Environmental planning attempts a very tricky balance between development and ecological sensitivity. Its supporters believe, however, that there is no reason why development and environmental protection cannot go hand-in-hand.

When the first European settlers arrived in North America, nature was generally conceived of as a force to be conquered by humans. Resources, such as freshwater, dense forests, and the American buffalo, were believed to be infinitely renewable. More than anything else, land was plentiful. The vast majority of the continent was not only uninhabited but unexplored by European settlers. Over time, settlers continued to move west, discovering a seemingly unlimited expanse of arable land (land that could be cultivated).

The belief that the country's natural resources were inexhaustible prevailed for some time, until the first conservationists began to advocate the preservation of natural resources—not out of an appreciation for the environment's inherent beauty, but for its economic potential. The environment needed to be carefully tended and harvested, rather than stripped bare. The national forestry movement was motivated by this developmental instinct. Wood is an excellent building material and a source of energy when burned, and for these reasons it became a protected resource. Trees in the national forests were treated like farm crops—planted every year only to be cut down. Forests, like farm fields, would be put on a cycle of harvesting and planting.

Other activists, influenced by the transcendentalist and romantic poets of the late nineteenth century, had more spiritual aims in mind. Nature, they argued, revitalized the human spirit, brought out the best in human endeavors, and provided numerous health benefits. The creation of the National Park Service in 1916, along with private activist organizations, such as the Sierra Club, which also advocated a more poetic, less materialistic appreciation of nature, foreshadowed the increasing role environmental activism would play in modern planning.

Following the Great Depression, the environmental movement in America focused on the rejuvenation of underdeveloped areas, such as the Tennessee Valley. While the advent of World War II temporarily interrupted the groundswell of environmental consciousness and refocused America's attention on the war effort, environmentalism has become a significant force in post-war American politics and public policy. The passage of the National Environmental Policy Act in 1969 and the celebration of the first Earth Day in 1970 attest to the fact that the conservationist movement has achieved popular acceptance.

Yet even Earth Day's international show of commitment to the environment failed to achieve across-the-board reforms. Conservation was up against the overwhelmingly powerful financial, political, and social forces of big business and development. In the 1970s and 1980s, however, several significant and well-publicized industrial accidents—including the partial meltdown of the Three Mile Island nuclear power plant, the discovery of chemical contamination at Love Canal, and the *Exxon Valdez* oil spill—spurred public interest in the environmental movement. And acts of civil disobedience on the part of environmental activists representing respected groups like Greenpeace generated admiration.

Under President Ronald Reagan, the environment received short shrift in favor of the pursuit of economic development. The only new environmental legislation he offered served to overturn previous environmental protection policy. Reagan's administration sought "regulatory reform." As discussed earlier, Reagan argued that the best way to revive a failing economy was to get rid of legislation that restricted the activities of private business and industry. Free to develop naturally, without the hindrance of government, the economy would thrive. In addition to the deregulation of business, Reagan began to phase out federally-subsidized planning programs and grants. In many ways, this policy was successful in jump-starting the economy. The very success of some of the country's business giants—among them oil companies and manufacturing plants—revived the country's concern for the environment, however. Many citizens began to doubt that these companies could be trusted to place concern for the environment over an interest in short-term profits.

By the end of Reagan's second term as president, environmental policy had once again been brought center stage, thanks to taxpayer skepticism and public outrage over environmental disasters. Some of the strongest environmental legislation was the product of this popular groundswell of support. New legislation made more rigorous demands of industry, focused the energies of environmental lobbies, and addressed some of the administrative obstacles to enforcing previous legislation.

While much of this legislation has been positive and worthwhile, many theorists make sure to note that America's new enthusiasm for protecting the environment has come during the period of great economic growth that characterized the Clinton era. Though the environmental movement stands in opposition to many of the practices of big business and industry and has many supporters of that stance, lawmakers will almost always side with business interests over environmental activists. Corporate America spends many millions of dollars on political campaigns in order to ensure that politicians friendly to their concerns and indebted to them for their support take office. Further, these companies employ millions of Americans. If complying with environmental regulations is seen as too costly for a company, it can threaten to layoff employees. These released workers are sure to take out their anger at the ballot box, voting against any politician who supported the pro-environment legislation. So among industrialists and average Americans alike, environmental concerns tend to get abandoned at the first sign of a weakening economy.

The Council on Environmental Quality (CEQ) and the Environmental Protection Agency (EPA) are the government watchdogs for environmental issues. As such, their primary purpose is to review the activities of other federal agencies (states have similar watchdogs to review the practices of state agencies). Under EPA regulations, all federal agencies must consider the environmental repercussions of all of their proposed projects. Prior to the approval of any federal project or any private project funded in part by a government agency, the acting party must complete an environmental impact statement (a study that details how the immediate environment will be affected by the proposed activity). The statement is completed in conjunction with other government agencies and with the involvement and input of the public (through public hearings, for example). The statement is for the benefit of the agency only; neither the EPA nor any other regulatory agency reviews the statement. It is intended merely to encourage agencies and the private companies working with them to consider the environmental consequences of their proposed actions, but it has no legal power to force them to put concerns for the environment ahead of their project. The statement simply serves to publicize the potential environmental issues surrounding a plan or project, and it forces government agencies to work with the public and maintain an attitude of negotiation and compromise.

Three areas of the environment receive the most publicity and require the most careful consideration by federal and state agencies: air, water, and waste. Addressing each of these issues is central to the work of environmental planning. An environmental planner might work to incorporate the existing natural environment into a plan for a local park, promenade, festival ground, or business district. An urban environmental planner might advise transportation engineers about the effects on the area's air quality and on the air quality of neighboring communities caused by a proposed highway or be asked to consider the role of privately-owned tollways in the lives of local residents. An urban planner might play a role in addressing a city's sewage treatment system, the capacity of rain gutters, and the effects of urban waste on local waterways and beaches. An urban planner might study the effects of a landfill or government-funded incentives proposed to encourage industries to recycle the by-products of their manufacturing plants. In such projects, the planner must consider ways to incorporate and protect the natural environment within the framework of state and federal environmental policy.

Transportation Planning

As discussed in chapter 1, the evolution of transportation in America was motivated by and, in turn, determined the course of urban settlement and suburban expansion. Motor vehicles have come to stand for independence, freedom, affluence, and that steroetypically American desire to explore the unknown by hitting the open road. Current figures attest to the overwhelming popularity of the automobile. At the end of the twentieth century, there were approximately 200 million operating automobiles in the United States. At least 90 percent of American households own an automobile, and half of all American households have two or more automobiles. On average, four out of five passenger cars on the road are occupied by only the driver. Public transit, for many years on the decline, has recently become more popular, but it still accounts for only 5 percent of commuter traffic.

Commuting patterns are changing as we enter the twenty-first century. In addition to the traditional commute (from suburb to city) and the less-common reverse commute (from city to suburb), a growing number of people are commuting from one suburb to another, shifting both the residential and business sectors still further away from the city. Furthermore, thanks to technological advances that make video conferencing and e-mail standard, more people are working at home, making a commute unnecessary. Though commuting is the subject of much of the research done on vehicular traffic, it accounts for only one in five trips made by the average American in his or her car. The social, ecological, and cultural effects of the automobile, with respect to commuting and the countless other reasons Americans choose to get in their cars, remains a central theme of urban planning.

Transportation planning is designed to combat the congestion, stress, and environmental repercussions of heavy vehicular traffic. It also tries to assure that people have easy access to public transit that will help them get to their places of employment. These aims have been addressed by a variety of theoretical plans and implemented programs.

Theoretically, the most dramatic changes to traffic patterns can be achieved by land use planning. By enforcing broad-based land use controls, government agencies could, to a great extent, regulate where people go by car and therefore the number of drivers on the road and how they use their cars. For example, one response to the overwhelming burdens placed on the highways by single occupancy vehicles is to build housing, particularly low-cost housing, near public transit stations and places of employment.

In addition, many planners advocate creating public and business areas, such as shopping malls and office parks, that serve multiple functions. They argue that when people work in single-use office environments, such as the sprawling office parks of the suburbs, they are obligated by their isolation to drive to work. They will also need their cars to drive to lunch, run errands, shop for groceries, or go to the bank. Where office environments incorporate other uses—stores, restaurants, banks—employees have easy access to these businesses without having to use a car. In addition, this variety ensures that the area will be used throughout the day by a regular stream of visitors. Less parking space is required, and the area is protected by the presence of many watchful eyes.

Land use planning faces administrative and public obstacles when applied to transportation issues, however. The government agencies responsible for land use and transportation are independent of each other and unlikely or unable to cooperate on projects. The employees of these two departments have different interests, skills, and administrative procedures. In addition, this kind of planning would require regional support, which is difficult to organize. Finally, it would be difficult to challenge the pattern of land use that holds traditional sway in a particular area. Change would be extremely slow and hard won.

The other avenue of action available to transportation planners is gaining direct control over the roadways, railways, skies, and seas traversed by American travelers. These projects often come under the heading "transportation demand management." Efforts to increase the available road space—by widening and lengthening existing roadways or building new roads altogether—have been unsuccessful in unclogging congestion. More new cars flood the roadways, probably in part because new space is made available. So the more roads and the wider the roads, the more traffic and congestion, not less. In addition, metropolitan areas face physical limitations and government restrictions on building new roads.

In several metropolitan centers, special highway lanes have been reserved for high occupancy vehicles (cars and trucks that hold more than two or three passengers). Traffic in these lanes generally moves faster because there are fewer cars. An added benefit is the reduction in pollution and gas consumption that results when fewer cars are on the road. Planners hope that the potential for a reduced travel time will encourage commuters and their employers to organize car pools. It is difficult, however, to monitor these lanes and hand out fines to single occupancy vehicles that use them illegally. Without the strict enforcement of fines, the program can become nearly useless. Other transportation management programs include the creation of shuttle services between neighborhoods and offices or shopping areas, the construction of showers and lockers in office buildings for employees who bike, run, or walk to work, and the building of park-and-ride lots adjoining public transit stations (so that a car is used only to get you as far as the nearest station and not all the way into the already crowded city on congested highways).

Another proposal is to place price controls on parking on the assumption that if parking becomes very expensive, commuters will leave their cars at home. One argument is to place restrictions on an employer's ability to offer free parking to its employees. It is estimated that it costs a commuter about $2,000 per year to park a single car in metropolitan Washington, D.C. By absorbing this cost, employers encourage single occupancy vehicle commuters and offer a monetary benefit to them that is denied to those who take public transit. Some transportation planners propose that this incentive system should be rearranged to target disadvantaged groups. They argue that those who take public transportation to work—not single occupancy car commuters—should be given a financial break.

In 1991, Congress passed the Intermodal Surface Transportation Efficiency Act. The act created the National Scenic Byways program, aimed at preserving and showcasing historic and natural landmarks. It also restructured the federal funding of transportation projects to address a broad range of issues at a time, rather than focus on individual projects. The act requires all states to formulate statewide transportation plans. Metropolitan areas are required to create metropolitan planning organizations, which must work in cooperation with state agencies. All programs must consider traffic congestion, work in conjunction with land use planning programs, study the effects of transportation policy on development programs, and work to create a unified system of private and public transportation. While the act does not provide local or state agencies with new authority, it serves to focus the efforts of these organizations.

Perhaps as tightly guarded by many Americans as the right to private ownership and free speech is the freedom of the open road. Cars have taken on mythic importance in American culture, which makes any transportation reform program that features restrictions or penalties on cars an extremely difficult endeavor. It is the role of the transportation planner, among other professionals, to create alternatives that are more cost-efficient, healthy, and ecologically sound than traditional, single occupancy automobile travel. The planner's even more difficult task is to separate Americans from their cars willingly, to make it seem like the most desirable option.

Historic Preservation

When something—a home, neighborhood, park, tavern, church, fort, or battlefield—is designated as a historic site, it becomes protected from alterations and development that would harm its traditional character. The scope and authority of historic preservation continues to grow. The earliest preservation efforts were made on behalf of individual sites dating from the seventeenth century to the early nineteenth century, such as the homes of former presidents at Mount Vernon and Monticello. Generally, these campaigns were undertaken by enthusiastic individuals or small historical societies that would buy structures or sites from private owners or the government and maintain them through private donations and government aid. Several pieces of important preservation legislation were passed in the first decades of the twentieth century. Each of these was intended to foster a spirit of cooperation in preserving culturally significant structures that were understood to have inspirational, historic, and educational value.

The urban renewal efforts of the 1950s and 1960s, which were marked by the demolition of business and residential areas—many of them of great historic

49

value—to make room for highways, skyscrapers, and public housing, gave rise to a new preservationist movement. In addition to sites of primarily cultural significance, preservationists began to focus their attention on architecturally significant structures. Not only did these sites serve academic or intellectual purposes, they were increasingly popular tourist destinations. In many cases, it became clear that the potential profit of demolishing and redeveloping a structure was outweighed by the profit that could be expected by rehabilitating a site and opening it to the public.

More often than not, however, rehabilitation is not immediately cost-effective. It can take years for a historic site to recoup the money spent on its renovations and ongoing maintenance and begin to turn a profit. Income from new development often pours in much more quickly. As a result, significant battles have been waged on all levels of government between individual development interests and the interests of numerous preservationist societies, organizations, and laws.

In the wake of the many regrettable demolitions that marked the mid-century urban renewal efforts, the legal framework within which preservationists operated changed, granting them more leverage in their constant struggle against developers. In 1966, the National Historic Preservation Act was passed, which included the creation of the National Register for Historic Places and the Advisory Council on Historic Preservation. The first organization is a comprehensive list of all neighborhoods, sites, structures, and objects that are significant in American history, culture, architectural history, engineering, or archaeological research. The second organization monitors government actions, reviewing proposed projects for their potential threat to historically and culturally significant areas or sites.

The National Environmental Policy Act (discussed earlier in this chapter) also serves as a federal review board. Environmental impact statements require federal agencies to consider the effects of actions or projects on "important historic, cultural, and natural aspects of our national heritage."

Throughout the late 1970s and 1980s, preservation efforts have also been supported at the federal level by tax incentives. Under the broad tax cuts of the early and mid-1980s, an average of 3,000 structural restoration or rehabilitation projects were undertaken each year. This activity slowed slightly following Reagan's 1986 tax reform package, which raised taxes, but there was still an average of 1,000 new projects each year. The late 1970s and the 1980s saw the rehabilitation of a total of 21,000 historic buildings with the help of tax incentives. The National Historic Preservation Act also granted federal money to state-run preservation projects, including the survey, planning, purchase, and development of historic sites.

At the state level, historic and cultural sites are theoretically protected by statewide preservation plans. Local and state agencies are supposed to work together to create comprehensive development plans that respect preservationist interests. Ideally, land use regulations, transportation development restrictions, and environmental protection, among other planning tools, would be used to help protect a site from demolition, damaging alterations, or encroachment by surrounding development. This process is overseen by the state historic preservation officer, who identifies and monitors historic sites across the state. Many municipalities also have the authority to designate the historical status of structures within their municipal boundaries and to regulate city development with respect to these landmarks.

As mentioned previously, this is the source of much conflict between developers on one side and municipal governments and preservationists on the other. In some cases, local municipalities are actually on the side of developers, tempted as they are by the tax dollars and job creation opportunities that a development project can bring. There is no guarantee that

The APA at Work: The Physically Active Community

The APA Research Department, with the help of a grant from the Robert Wood Johnson Foundation, is conducting research and preparing educational materials on planning and designing communities that encourage physical activity and healthy living among its residents. The focus of the study is on "smart" community development that encourages walking, bicycling, and other forms of daily physical activity. This can be achieved by the building of parks, the construction of bike and walking paths, the providing of non-automobile transportation options, and the formation of various fitness and recreation clubs, among many other options.

a town or city government will recognize, appreciate, and cherish the valuable and threatened sites within its jurisdiction.

The preservation legislation of the late 1960s has shifted the balance of power between developers and preservationists. Today, historic preservation is a broad term that can encompass a wide range of sites and objects. Historic status is bestowed upon everything from individual relics to fragments of rooms to buildings to entire city districts. The chronological scope of the preservation movement has expanded to include anything from artifacts of ancient civilizations to modern skyscrapers that are less than fifty years old.

Planners work to develop districtwide, citywide, and regionwide plans that protect and cultivate an area's historic character while adapting to the forward-thinking trends in economic and transportation development. They study urban webs, breaking a city down into neighborhoods, blocks, and parcels, making it easier to target certain historic sites. They work to maintain the visual continuity of a neighborhood by cooperating with architects and designers on new developments, ensuring that new construction or renovations do not radically differ in character and style from the established buildings. The philosophy of preservation planning is that by studying the historic and cultural character of an area and working to maintain it, planning can strengthen the underlying structures of a community. A city that respects and values its past, the theory goes, will have greater care for its present and future, too. Preservation is a way of revitalizing a city and sustaining its livelihood.

Aesthetics

The consideration of aesthetics—a branch of philoso-phy dealing with the nature of beauty, art, and taste—is closely related to land use planning, environmental pro-tection, community development, and historic preser-vation. The history of city beautification has been suggested in discussions of each of the previous spe-cializations and in the history of cities outlined in chapter 2. This section will focus on a specific aesthetic question facing modern planners.

Aesthetics and the right of a governmental body to determine what is aesthetically pleasing first became a matter for judicial review with the appearance of adver-tising billboards. Billboards require special zoning for their construction. In the early 1900s, municipal ordi-nances in several American cities attempted to control the appearance of billboards by requiring that they be placed a certain distance from the road. Billboard owners filed suit, arguing that the city had no right to regulate the appearance of a privately owned structure. The courts initially found the city ordinances unconsti-tutional, arguing that appearances were a luxury or indulgence and did not fall under the scope of the city's authority. Opinions shifted over time, however.

By the 1930s, the courts had become convinced that appearances could help determine the character of a place by setting a certain tone. Soon, billboards were being blamed for lapses in morality and public decency. Billboards, it came to be thought, were a threat to public health and safety. They were poorly constructed and threatened the safety of buildings and individuals nearby. They were not only unattractive, they were offensive. Their owners corrupted our political system by offering free advertising space to campaigning officials in return for special favors. They provided hiding places for criminals and misbehaving young people. At least, these were the arguments made in newspapers, town halls, and courtrooms.

It was eventually determined that the city had the right to regulate aesthetics as part of a larger attempt to protect its residents from various social and cultural evils. For example, in New York in the early 1930s, the state constructed a screen along a stretch of highway to block the motorists' views of the surrounding area. A billboard had been erected that threatened the safety of drivers, who might be distracted by its presence. The billboard's owner filed suit, arguing that the state had completely devalued his private investment without compensating him for it. The court upheld the state's right to build the screen, stating that the billboard's owner had no investment in the road and no legal claim that his billboard be seen from it.

Over the following decades, the city's authority was extended beyond billboards to include residential appearance codes, design guidelines, and landscape regulations. As a result, owning a home or building no longer meant that one had near total freedom to do with the property as one wished. Today, these design guidelines vary greatly from one city to another. Most cities lack coherent design plans, and it is unclear whether those that exist are working. Many are too vague to effectively regulate development. Others are criticized as imposing excessively strict standards of regularity and continuity (creating bland, uniform city streets) or, on the other extreme, excessively strict standards of dissimilarity (leading to a riot of building styles that lacks any unity). In either case, some critics argue that these guidelines stifle creativity and experimentation and result in the mundane and predictable. Aesthetic concerns play a significant role in creating a livable environment, and effective ways to encourage interesting, visually pleasing construction are still being developed and tested.

The Planner as Social Advocate

Urban planners are first and foremost professionals and masters of a creative and technical skill. They are also, however, members of a community. They must recognize their role as social advocates and their obligations to not only their communities and clients, but to their society as a whole. As discussed in detail earlier, planners can act as advocates for the socially and economically disadvantaged through equity and community development planning. Yet these are not the only tools on hand. As suggested before, the specializations available to an urban planner are not clearly distinct and independent of one another, either in philosophy or practice. A planner can attempt to champion the interests of the disadvantaged through a combination of land use, environment, equity, community development, transportation, preservation, and aesthetic planning. The overriding goal of urban planning is not merely to lay down streets, put up buildings, and move people around like chess pieces. It is to create livable, harmonious, healthy, prosperous communities. Indeed, an urban planner can have as direct an effect upon the lives of a city's disadvantaged residents as any social worker, doctor, or politician.

Is Urban Planning Right for You?

4

A job that builds on the strengths and interests of one person might be completely unsuited to someone else's personality and talents. Within the set parameters of a job description, it is often possible to take on more responsibilities or branch out into new directions that best suit your skills and enthusiasms. To make the most of yourself, however, you need to find the right job. Deciding on a career will be one of the most important decisions you make in life. So it is important to gain an accurate sense of your interests, talents, and desires and get as much information as possible about your prospective career.

Qualities of a Successful Planner

Understanding what it takes to become an urban planner will help you decide if it is the right kind of job for you. Consider the characteristics outlined in the following section and compare them with your own system of beliefs, skills and weaknesses, interests and inclinations. Do you share the qualities of a successful planner?

First, planners must have a desire to improve their surroundings. As discussed in the previous chapter, planners are often social advocates, which requires an interest in the people and places beyond your own backyard. Planners must be able to understand and evaluate a complex web of social problems, controversies, and competing wishes, while maintaining an objective perspective. They must be interested in addressing these issues and taking some responsibility for their solutions. However, it is not the role of the urban planner to enforce his or her own moral, cultural, or social beliefs on a community—quite the opposite. Planners must honestly study what makes a community unique and consider ways to build on these intrinsic strengths. Implicit in this endeavor is willingness on the part of the planner to listen to many different kinds of people, respect their opinions, and make judgments about what will work and what will not.

Planners must be interested in exploring the physical design of cities and communities, placing this design in the context of a larger history of urban development, and analyzing trends and theories of urban growth and decay. This requires a basic understanding of how cities work—a familiarity with neighborhoods, transportation systems, public utilities, local and citywide government structures, site-specific environmental concerns, special interest groups, and the community's demographic makeup. Planners must be willing to collect data from a variety of sources, analyze it, draw conclusions, formulate opinions, and do their best to predict an area's economic, political, and cultural future. A planner must also be able to determine immediate, short-term, and long-term goals. A planner, then, needs to be a skilled communicator, mathematician, analyst, theorist, judge, and social forecaster.

The ability to work with a variety of people within his or her professional community, including architects, designers, accountants, economists, and lawyers, is essential to a successful planner. Planners must be conversant in the specialized vocabulary of each of these professions and capable of integrating each of their varied perspectives into the final proposal. In addition, planners must be willing to take advice and criticism from these trained professionals.

Planners must be technically skilled, combining a knowledge of engineering, geography, and planning-oriented computer programs. They also must be creative and experimental, able to come up with new ideas, designs, and solutions, and represent them effectively in sketches, models, and written proposals.

Serving in the role of mediator, negotiator, and representative of unpopular opinions is a common practice for planners. As such, the planner must be able to manage conflict and serve as an effective diplomat, trying to create common ground and consensus between opposing factions. He or she must also be a skilled communicator and public speaker, able to converse comfortably with a wide range of people. Perhaps most important, planners must be able to translate their plans and ideas into easily understandable terms and concepts for a less knowledgeable audience of politicians and community members. Planners must be opinionated but respectful, persistent but polite.

For example, citizens opposed to a mall going up in their backyard, which could drive their property values down and decrease their quality of life, will exert pressure to kill the project. On the other hand, politicians and town officials interested in the tax income and jobs generated by a mall will probably throw their influence behind the project. Joining them would be citizens living further away from the project area who want the new shopping and job opportunities the mall has to offer. Opposed to them will be local store owners who will feel threatened by the competition offered by the larger, wealthier chain stores that will move into the mall and cut into their business. Wading into these troubled waters, as an urban planner must, requires great tact, patience, diplomacy, compromise, peacemaking, and problem-solving abilities.

A planner must be able to evaluate the impact his or her choices have had on the world at large and, most important, the targeted community. Planners study their successes and their failures and apply these real-world lessons to subsequent endeavors. As such, planners must be willing to admit error, accept criticism, and forget grudges. Planners must regularly reinvent themselves and revise their notions of what works, adapting their plans to the growing body of theory and practice in the professional planning community and to changing times. There is a regular influx of new projects, new theories, and idealistic young newcomers, so a planner must remain adaptable and engaged in current trends in order to continue to succeed and thrive.

How do your expectations, desires, and personality match up with these generalizations about the qualities necessary for a successful planner? Do you have a

Checklist of a Planner's Skills

❒ A planner must understand the way a city is designed and how all its various parts work.

❒ A planner must be able to compile, read, and understand information on population, employment, health, and other trends.

❒ A planner must include a wide range of people in making decisions and be able to maintain their support for a project. He or she must also be able to speak to a wide variety of people so that they understand what is involved.

❒ A planner must understand the inner workings of local, state, and federal governments, especially how they decide to commit money and energy to a project. He or she must also be familiar with the legal implications and requirements of a given project.

❒ A planner must not only understand how a project will affect a community but also take responsibility for its impact.

❒ A planner must consider the ways in which the economy, transportation systems, health and human services, and zoning regulations mesh when devising a community development plan.

strong interest in improving the lives of city residents? Are you fascinated by the intricate workings of a city? Do you have the ability to master a wide range of technical information covering several fields? Can you move easily between different groups of people and build agreements among them? Are you adaptable, open to suggestions, and interested in the latest developments? If the answer to all these questions is yes, then you are an excellent candidate for this kind of work. Having determined your interest in and suitability for this kind of work, you are now ready to begin taking the steps necessary to prepare for your career in urban planning.

The APA at Work: Neighborhood Collaborative Planning

Funded by the Annie E. Casey Foundation, this project encourages planners to think about how the lives of children and families—especially those of the disadvantaged—can be improved through planning. Neighborhood Collaborative Planning seeks to increase the overall health of a neighborhood by involving the full range of community components that can affect families and children in all planning decisions. Health and human services, education, crime prevention, and economic development are all taken into consideration, and the input of community development organizations is encouraged.

The Planner's Salary

Salary is an important consideration when choosing a career. It is a good idea to have realistic expectations of how much you are likely to make in a given career over time. This knowledge will enable you to make other decisions about your home, family, lifestyle, and retirement. Since you are interested in establishing a career in planning, you will no doubt also want to be able to accurately plan for your future.

Urban planners are generally well paid. Figures vary depending on the nature of the organization (whether it is government-run, private, or nonprofit), the work experience of the employee, and the city and state in which the employee works. Generally, planners working in federal agencies, law firms, and development corporations have the highest salaries in the profession. Planners working for county or regional agencies and nonprofit organizations have the lowest salaries in the field. Still, the median salary for planners in these organizations is over $40,000, well above the salaries of non-professionals and national averages.

The following table, based on figures gathered by the American Planning Association (APA) in 1998, gives an indication of the salary range for planners of different degrees of experience, living and working in different states. For example, the median salary for an urban planner with more than ten years of experience working in the Washington, D.C., area is $94,500, which suggests the high earning potential of professional federal employees, most of whom work in the nation's capital.

Planners' Median Salaries
by State and Years of Experience (1998)

Experience	5 Years	5 to 10 Years	More Than 10 Years
State			
Alabama	30,200	40,900	53,200
Alaska	41,500	83,000	57,700
Arizona	27,900	43,600	65,600
Arkansas	39,900	37,300	51,400
California	36,900	51,800	74,300
Colorado	35,000	43,700	56,800
Connecticut	31,700	46,900	64,100
Delaware	30,600	45,900	68,300
District of Columbia	44,000	49,700	94,500
Florida	31,400	41,500	59,400
Georgia	30,800	38,600	53,000
Hawaii	32,800	41,300	75,400
Idaho	37,700	34,400	43,900
Illinois	32,800	45,900	61,000
Indiana	30,700	37,200	44,300
Iowa	26,200	38,000	56,800
Kansas	31,700	36,100	57,000
Kentucky	27,000	31,700	43,700
Louisiana	26,200	41,000	49,000
Maine	32,800	39,900	39,900
Maryland	33,900	44,000	60,300
Massachusetts	37,200	46,700	65,600
Michigan	35,500	42,400	55,100
Minnesota	33,500	44,100	56,800
Mississippi	28,000	36,600	41,600
Missouri	29,000	40,400	66,700
Montana	21,900	39,300	44,800
Nebraska	35,800	41,900	51,500

Experience	5 Years	5 to 10 Years	More Than 10 Years
State			
Nevada	38,700	44,800	71,000
New Hampshire	30,500	36,100	52,800
New Jersey	38,200	46,400	69,900
New Mexico	30,300	38,200	53,500
New York	39,300	47,400	65,500
North Carolina	39,700	38,900	52,300
North Dakota	34,600	32,800	46,300
Ohio	31,700	41,100	54,700
Oklahoma	30,000	44,000	55,700
Oregon	35,000	39,900	56,300
Pennsylvania	28,500	38,200	53,500
Rhode Island	37,600	45,700	48,200
South Carolina	30,800	38,200	48,600
South Dakota	32,800	41,600	43,700
Tennessee	30,400	37,700	54,600
Texas	37,200	43,300	61,100
Utah	31,000	37,400	56,800
Vermont	NA	38,200	42,200
Virginia	34,400	43,200	59,300
Washington	37,800	47,200	61,200
West Virginia	40,600	38,700	46,800
Wisconsin	33,400	43,000	53,500
Wyoming	NA	36,800	42,300

Salaries differ considerably depending on whether you are employed by a private company, nonprofit organization, or a government agency (and if in government, whether you are employed at the local, state, or federal level). The following table, provided by the APA, lists median salaries by employer.

Planners' Median Salaries by Employer (1998)

City	49,700
County	43,700
Joint City/County	45,700
Metro/Regional	43,400
State Provincial	47,500
Federal Government	65,600
Economic Development	48,600
Private Consultant	56,600
Nonprofit Organization	45,300
Educational Institution	59,900
Law Firm	65,700
Development Firm	82,000
Other Public Agency	53,500
Other Private Agency	54,600

While your salary as a planner may never reach as high as those of some of your friends who entered more high-profile professions, such as law or medicine, you will receive much in the way of intangible compensation, such as the opportunity to put your ideals into practice and see your ideas leap from the drawing board into reality.

How to Become an Urban Planner

Becoming a qualified urban planner will require a strong educational foundation. You will have to attend school for several years and most likely get a higher degree (a master's or Ph.D.). Since you will be spending so much time in school, and since your degree is so important to your job prospects, it is especially important that you choose a school that is both right for you and offers a course of study appropriate to a planning career.

Education Requirements and the Career Path

While urban planning firms and city agencies hire a diverse group of people from many disciplines and educational backgrounds, most professional urban planners are college graduates with master's or Ph.D. degrees in areas such as urban planning, economic development, or architecture. Federal, state, and local government planning agencies generally require at least a master's degree in urban or regional planning, urban design, or the equivalent work experience for most jobs. While you may be able to get an entry-level position with only a bachelor's degree in planning, architecture, engineering, or design, your lack of professional training and specialized knowledge will be an obstacle to your speedy advancement within the organization.

A bachelor's degree from an accredited planning program, coupled with a master's degree in architecture, landscape architecture, or civil engineering, is good preparation for entry-level planning jobs in areas such as urban design, transportation, or the environment. A master's degree from an accredited planning program at a good school provides the best training for a number of different planning fields. Although graduates from one of the limited number of accredited bachelor's degree programs qualify for many entry-level positions, their advancement opportunities are often limited unless they acquire an advanced degree. Courses in related disciplines such as architecture, law, earth sciences, demography, economics, finance, health administration, geographic information systems, and management are highly recommended. In addition, familiarity with computer models and statistical techniques is necessary.

With a degree and a certain amount of work experience, planners can take an examination administered by the American Institute of Certified Planners (AICP) and be granted professional certification upon passing. Membership in and accreditation from professional organizations like AICP can help you advance in your career, learn of job openings, gain access to people in a position to hire, network with colleagues, and stay on top of the latest developments in your field.

After a few years of experience, planners may advance to assignments requiring a high degree of independent judgment and creativity, such as designing the physical layout of a large development or recommending policy and budget options that will help a proposed project become a reality. Some public sector planners are promoted to community planning director and spend a great deal of time meeting with officials, speaking to civic groups, and supervising a staff. Further advancement occurs through a transfer to a larger jurisdiction with more complex problems and greater responsibilities, or into related occupations, such as director of community or economic development.

Graduate Programs

Graduate degrees in urban planning incorporate a study of the history of cities, an exploration of new urban planning theories and methods, experimentation with the technical and analytical instruments of the profession, and often an in-depth investigation of one of the specialized planning disciplines (such as transportation or land use planning).

A sample course schedule from a two-year graduate program in urban planning might include the following core classes: Analytic Methods in Planning, The Economics of Policy Analysis, The History and Theories of Planning, Legal Precedents and Modern Applications of Land Use Planning, and Field Problems in Planning.

In addition, electives in the following disciplines might be offered: Applied Geographical Information Systems (GIS) in Planning Analysis, Spatial Analysis in Planning, Social Equity Planning, Growth Management, and Project Impact Analysis. These course titles might sound intimidating, but they simply represent different ways of tackling some of the complex issues that are raised by typical urban planning projects. Despite their off-putting titles, most of the courses are devoted to the kind of problem solving you will perform every day as a planner. In essence, they address how to develop projects given the limitations imposed by geography, budgets, zoning restrictions, environmental concerns, and community objections.

A graduate urban planning program teaches the student how to think critically and comprehensively about the way people live, work, and play. It pays particular attention to how these behaviors constitute a social fabric that affects hundreds of other people every day. In addition, a graduate planning program teaches the student how to apply theory and manipulate technical instruments in an effort to propose solutions to inefficiencies or failures in the social fabric (by, for example, installing speed bumps on a residential street plagued by speeding motorists or creating lush landscaping for a new shopping center in an otherwise blighted neighborhood). Finally, a graduate planning program teaches the student how to review a plan that has been implemented, analyzing its impact on the community as a whole and the specific group it was meant to serve, determining its strengths and flaws, and measuring its degree of success.

Schools with Planning Programs Accredited by the Planning Accreditation Board

Alabama A&M University

Arizona State University

Ball State University

California Polytechnic State University, San Luis Obispo

California State Polytechnic University, Pomona

Clemson University

Cleveland State University

Columbia University

Cornell University

Eastern Michigan University

Eastern Washington University

Florida Atlantic University

Florida State University

Georgia Institute of Technology

Harvard University

Hunter College, City University of New York

Iowa State University

Kansas State University

Massachusetts Institute of Technology

Michigan State University

Morgan State University

(continued on page 72)

(continued from page 71)

New York University
Ohio State University
Portland State University
Pratt Institute
Rutgers, The State University of New Jersey
San Jose State University
State University of New York, Albany
State University of New York, Buffalo
Texas A&M University
University of Arizona
University of British Columbia
University of California, Berkeley
University of California, Irvine
University of California, Los Angeles
University of Cincinnati
University of Colorado, Denver
University of Florida
University of Hawaii, Manoa
University of Illinois, Chicago
University of Illinois, Urbana-Champaign
University of Iowa
University of Kansas
University of Maryland, College Park
University of Massachusetts, Amherst

University of Memphis
University of Michigan
University of Minnesota
Université de Montréal
University of Nebraska, Lincoln
University of New Mexico
University of New Orleans
University of North Carolina, Chapel Hill
University of Oklahoma
University of Oregon
University of Pennsylvania
University of Puerto Rico
University of Rhode Island
University of Southern California
University of Tennessee, Knoxville
University of Texas, Arlington
University of Texas, Austin
University of Virginia
University of Washington
University of Wisconsin, Madison
University of Wisconsin, Milwaukee
Virginia Commonwealth University
Virginia Polytechnic Institute and State University
Wayne State University

Admissions Requirements

While many graduate programs in urban planning do not require applicants to have completed undergraduate degrees in urban studies, architecture, or related fields, many undergraduate institutions offer these classes, and they can provide superb introductions to the planning field. The offerings and requirements of undergraduate and graduate planning programs vary widely, and applicants are encouraged to do extensive research when choosing a planning program to guarantee they choose the one most closely suited to their needs and interests.

Undergraduate institutions generally require students to complete the SAT or ACT, provide high school transcripts and recommendations from teachers or guidance counselors, and fill out an extensive application that may include an essay. Information on these procedures and the requisite steps required by individual institutions can be obtained from guidance counselors, college Web sites, or the college directly. You may also contact the institution's admissions office directly for more information.

Admissions requirements for graduate institutions will differ slightly from one planning program to another. You will probably need to take the Graduate Record Examination (GRE) and have your scores reported to the institutions to which you are applying. This exam tests your analytical and verbal abilities, in addition to several elective, subject-specific tests. Practice exams and test-taking strategies can be found in books, on the Internet, and in preparatory seminars. As is the case in the undergraduate admissions process, you will have to complete an application, request recommendations from professors or employers, and, often, write a statement of purpose outlining your academic interests, proposed course of study, and professional ambitions.

In addition, many graduate programs require the completion of undergraduate course work in particular areas of the planning field. If you have not completed this course work at your undergraduate institution, you may still be able to apply to the graduate program and make up the course work either before beginning your studies or during the course of your program. Refer to the program's admissions materials or ask an admissions officer for more information. Admissions materials for both undergraduate and graduate institutions may also provide estimates for the mean grade point average of those candidates that have been accepted in the past, as well as showcase the portfolios (the body of work created in class, extracurricularly during their college education, or through work experience) of successful applicants. This will help give you a better idea of what level of work is required for admission and how strong your chances are, as well as how well you compare to previously accepted applicants.

Choosing a Program

The undergraduate and graduate school application process is a complex one. Before you request applications, write essays, and pay processing fees, give yourself several months to research your selected career and the schools and programs that offer undergraduate or graduate education in urban planning, architecture, design, or engineering. Here are some tips to help guide you through the process of choosing a school.

First, read about real-life planners, planning projects, and the history of planning theory. The For Further Reading section at the back of this book will get you started. Consult the bibliographies and references listed in each of these books to expand your knowledge even further, and visit your local library, where books on planning and planning theory can be found under the headings of urban studies, art history, and even biography. Visit the Web site (listed at the back of this book) of the American Planning Association for recent developments in planning, and explore the countless other planning-oriented Web sites.

Next, consider your own strengths and weaknesses, your social, cultural, and political interests, and the kinds of academic environments in which you thrive. Make a list of the aspects of planning that particularly interest you, and compare your list to the main themes addressed in the school's literature for prospective students and in the most recent course catalog. What particular areas of planning and types of planning projects spark your interest? Does the school offer classes in these areas? Does the school offer any special programs that cater to a more hands-on approach to learning, by offering work-study programs or internships, for example?

Get to know the ins and outs of prospective programs. What courses are offered and which ones are required for your area of study? Does the school accept transfer students? Can you defer enrollment if you are accepted? Does the faculty include practicing urban planners, in addition to full-time professors? In what area does each faculty member specialize? Do these areas match your particular planning interests? Are they looking for a certain kind of candidate—for example, engineering majors, those who concentrate on environmental issues, or candidates with strong volunteer experience? Do you match up well with the kind of applicant they seem to desire? What kinds of students are currently enrolled in the program? Are they younger or older? Campus residents or commuters? Do you want a classic college experience, featuring dorm living and campus activities, or would being a "day student" be more suitable? Does the program feature a racially and economically diverse student body? Do its graduates go on to successful careers with major firms and government agencies?

Consider all of the school's facilities. Explore its library. Research its other graduate programs, such as geography, environmental management, and political science, and find out if you are eligible to take classes in these other disciplines. Consider the town or city where the school is located. Is it the right size, climate, and environment for you? Try to picture yourself on the campus of each school you read about or visit.

Through the alumni or graduate placement office or your personal connections, make contact with recent program graduates. What are they doing now? How did they choose their area of specialization, their employer, or their work environment? How did their educational experiences prepare them for their current employment? What do they consider to be the strengths and weaknesses of the program? What information about the program should you know that cannot be found in the admissions literature? As with all informational interviews, this should be a dialogue. Share relevant information about your own experiences and plans for the future. If people know something about your own goals, they will be better equipped to advise you on the best course of action for achieving them and helping you determine if the program is well suited to your interests.

Finally, research the likely cost of attending the program, including not only tuition, but housing, transportation, food, textbooks, and research materials. Contact a financial aid representative and learn more about scholarship packages and financial aid. What percentage of the students receive financial aid? Do scholarships

The APA at Work: The City Parks Forum

With the City Parks Forum, the APA collaborates, shares information, and exchanges ideas with mayors across the country about park issues and the ways in which urban parks can improve the quality of life and prosperity of city residents and businesses. Through a series of symposia held across the country, the APA seeks to convince mayors of the importance of developing parks, emphasizing how parks provide valuable community gathering places, boost property values, offer city residents a therapeutic space in which to reconnect with nature, and create a more inviting—and therefore profitable—city for residents and tourists alike.

cover all or only part of tuition and living expenses? How much money in student loans can you receive, and what are the terms of repayment? Are any work-study, campus jobs, teaching assistantships, or paying internships available to help defray the costs of tuition?

The Application Process

When you have thoroughly researched a number of institutions and considered your own potential as a candidate, you are finally ready to begin the application process. Allow yourself several months to compile all of the requisite materials, and be sure your application arrives on time.

Contact the school about scheduling an interview on campus or with an admissions representative in your area. This is an ideal opportunity to put your best foot forward and will give you an advantage over the applicants who opt not to have an interview. Interviews offer a valuable chance to reveal the personality and passion behind the name on the application, to put a human face on the document that is otherwise like thousands of other applications. Admissions interviews often allow for an easy dialogue. After all, you are talking about something you know a lot about—yourself!

Before the interview, try to predict some of the questions that the interviewer will ask and construct the basic framework of your answers. Avoid memorizing heavily scripted responses, however; without some spontaneity, you may come across as insincere. This is your opportunity to share your enthusiasm for urban planning with your prospective school. Acknowledge your weaknesses, demonstrate a determination to work on them, and assert your strengths. You are applying for an educational program, which means you aren't expected to know everything already. Be honest, eager, polite, and, above all, relaxed.

Get Involved Now

6

If you are interested in exploring any of the specialties described in this book, including architecture, design, planning, community development, conservation, and preservation, the opportunities to do so in your own community are endless. You can begin immediately, without waiting to reach college first. Early, firsthand, practical experience with the aspects of planning that intrigue you will also help you test your abilities and interest level before committing to a course of study or career path.

In the Classroom

Your high school may offer classes in technical drawing, architecture, art history, economics, public policy, or urban design. Often these sorts of electives are a high school's best-kept secret, so ask your guidance counselor for more information, and take advantage of any courses that will give you an introduction to the fundamental elements of the practice of urban planning. Contact a local university or community college and request information on summer, night, or weekend courses that relate to planning. Many colleges and universities offer extensive continuing education courses for teens and adults on topics as diverse as the history and theories of planning, the basics of technical drawing, and an introduction to computer-based planning programs. Courses in urban design and community development will prepare you for the educational challenges you will face as you pursue your degree. They will also introduce you to new ideas and enhance your résumé. You might even be able to visit graduate level classes and observe project critiques, talk to students and professors, and get a sense of what an education in planning would entail in terms of work load, intellectual stimulation, creative expression, and hands-on experience.

At the Museum

Visit your local museum, library, historical society, parks department, or historic site to find out about educational seminars, lectures, weekend activities, exhibits, special archives, and volunteer opportunities. These public institutions may also offer you a practical, living lesson in urban planning by providing valuable information about how they were financed and built and how they are currently maintained, funded, and utilized by members of the community.

Consider, for example, one of the foremost American museums for the study of architecture, engineering, design, construction, and urban planning: the National Building Museum in Washington, D.C. The National Building Museum is a nonprofit organization created in 1980 and housed in the formidable, nineteenth-century building originally occupied by the U.S. Pension Bureau. The building itself is a testament to remarkable architectural skill and is a showcase of American urban beautification efforts of the 1880s.

The Great Hall resembles an Italian piazza (plaza), with a central fountain, seventy-five-foot Corinthian columns at both ends, and two tiers of repeated arches, which resemble ornate Roman aqueducts, lining opposite walls. The walls on either side of these are crowned with a row of windows, through which sunlight pours down and decorates the floor with a complex pattern of light and shade.

This is an inspirational, awe-inspiring place to study architecture, and members of the community take advantage of the museum's extensive calendar of events. There are programs aimed at families, adults, and children. The building bustles with the activity of area school children on field trips participating in programs such as Wonders of Wood, Fuller's Fantastic Geodesic Dome, and Patterns that Thump, Bump, and Jump. In the afternoons, museum guides lead tours of special exhibits and the building itself. In the evenings, lectures and symposia offer educational opportunities for adults.

In addition, the museum offers several programs aimed just at teens. Investigating Where We Live is a five-week program for young adults. Participants are given an introduction to photography and then sent out onto the streets of particular neighborhoods to document the local communities while learning about each neighborhood's history from course instructors. At the end of the program, students prepare a museum exhibit of their images and ideas.

City Vision is another of the museum's programs. It is aimed at the youth of Washington's inner city. Under the mentorship of planning professionals and students from surrounding colleges and universities, the high schoolers are first taught basic design principles and technical skills, including sketching and model building. Having laid this basic foundation, the course then focuses on the "finesse" skills of communication, negotiation, diplomacy, and social and political advocacy. Finally, students take their new expertise to the streets, analyzing communities from social, economic, and design perspectives and suggesting ways in which problems can be solved. Drawing on this research and observation, the students create a structured presentation of the design problems they have identified and their proposed solutions. The presentation is complete with models, slides, and drawings. The audience, made up in part by professional planners, community leaders, and designers, is given the opportunity to ask questions and engage the students in a dialogue about their ideas. In all, City Vision is a three-month commitment, and students from five area middle schools participate each year.

The National Building Museum is an important resource, helping visitors learn more about what makes a community a livable environment. While it may be one of the more impressive examples of museums dedicated to architecture and urban planning, it is not the only one. Look into museums and historical societies in your community and take advantage of the similar educational programming they provide.

On the Job

One of the most educationally and professionally enriching experiences one can gain is through an internship. It is important, in considering any career, to observe professionals on the job, doing exactly the kind of work that you hope to do someday. Do you like the feel of office work? The pace and personality of the organization? What are some of the drawbacks of an office setting? What are some of the benefits? Contact urban planning associations, private firms, nonprofit organizations, or government commissions in your area, and apply for internships (which may be paid or unpaid) or offer your services as a volunteer.

An internship can provide a student or recent graduate with the opportunity to try out different jobs and work environments. It is a great way to make contacts within a field, which can be used when applying for summer programs, college or graduate school, or career-track jobs. In addition, many internships include some form of payment or stipend to cover living and commuting expenses. Consider internships in your own neighborhood, in nearby cities, and even in foreign countries. Research North American–based employment or work abroad agencies that place young people in foreign work environments as interns or volunteers. You have the opportunity to explore a different culture while also enhancing your résumé and greatly enriching your work experience.

Doing Your Homework

When approaching organizations or businesses for the first time, be sure to do your homework. Do not flip through the phone book and send a form letter to every entry listed under the heading Urban Planning. Your letter should reflect some special familiarity with that particular company, such as its size, philosophical approach, and recent and renowned projects. It should not be worded in such a broad way that its recipient can tell that it has been sent to two dozen similar companies with only the names and addresses being changed.

While it is important to explore a broad base of businesses and organizations, some discretion is recommended. At the library or online, research your target organizations and businesses. There's no point in making extra work for yourself by writing to companies for which you have no real interest in working. For example, you enter the phrase "urban planning" into an Internet search engine, which connects you to, among countless others, the homepage of ABC Planning, which is located in your hometown of Metropolis, U.S.A. Familiarize yourself with ABC's mission statement, its past projects, and its staff. Do they have a particular environmental, social, economic, or political agenda? If so, do you sympathize with it, or does it contradict your own principles?

Once you have made yourself familiar with ABC's work, ask yourself if you think the company's projects have been successful. Have they fulfilled their expectations? Has the community been positively affected? What do you think works about the projects? What does not work? Investigate how large the company is and how many of the employees are licensed planners. Get an idea for how closely associated the company is with the academic community by finding out how many of the employees also teach at the local college and university and publish articles in trade magazines, academic journals, or scholarly books. This information may indicate how cutting edge the company is and how involved in the latest planning trends and theories. You may also want to learn how much community outreach they perform, by giving talks at schools and libraries, donating their time, energy, and ideas to neighborhood improvement initiatives (like building houses for Habitat for Humanity, for example), or offering scholarships to inner-city children interested in careers in planning.

Making Contact

If the company's Web site does not provide adequate answers to these and other questions, do not hesitate to ask them in the course of an informational interview. An informational interview is an interview given by someone working in the field to someone hoping to break in. It generally does not lead to a job offer but is meant only to give you the chance to gain the information you need to plan your education and plot your career path. It is surprising how willing many people are to grant informational interviews. Many professionals received them when they were starting out and feel it is their responsibility to return the favor and cultivate the next generation. It helps, however, if you have a contact (such as a relative or friend of a family member) in the company who can grant you an interview or put you in touch with someone who will. Remember, successful interviews are conversations, not interrogations or sales pitches. It is important to show potential employers that you have an able and active mind, that you have familiarized yourself with the company or organization, that you can listen as well as speak, and that you are eager to learn more, preferably on the job.

When contacting an organization or firm for the first time, it is best to address your inquiry to a specific person, rather than the organization or company as a whole. For example, try to avoid addressing a letter to "To Whom It May Concern." If possible, make contacts with professional preservationists, conservationists, and planners before you begin your search. Ask these industry insiders for the names of firms and individuals who might provide useful information on the planning profession and help you get on-the-job experience as an intern or volunteer (these are questions that can also be asked during your informational interview). Find the names of notable planners working in your area by perusing city or regional planning journals, researching the development of neighborhoods that have piqued your interest, and searching the Internet. In a brief, straightforward letter, outline your interest in the profession, your experience thus far, and your plans for the future.

First, consider the following letter, written by fictitious high school senior John Smith to regional planner Jane Doe.

John Smith
200 Crown Street
Metropolis, State 10010
February 1, 2003

Jane Doe
ABC Planning
300 Front Street
Metropolis, State 10010

Dear Ms. Doe:

I love urban planning! I'd like to learn more about ABC
Planning. How many people work there? What is the office
atmosphere like? Are you hiring any interns this summer?

    I have a lot of experience, which I think would make
me an ideal candidate for a position in your company. All of
my experience, both in and out of the classroom, has given
me a unique perspective and a strong desire to learn more. I
have come to believe that planning is the single most
important way for people to improve their invironments,
prepare for the future, and create a better world for our
children.

    I would like to talk to you more about planning, pref-
farrably during the week of March 17th. Please call me at
222-7777 as soon as possible to set up a meeting.

Sincerely,
John Smith

John's letter is riddled with vague assertions, trite sentiments, and spelling errors. He offers none of the concrete details concerning his experience that might make Jane Doe view him as a promising candidate, instead insisting, in a very informal tone, that he "loves urban planning!" John poses questions about company size, work environment, and availability of internships to which he should already know the answers. If the information was not available on the company's Web site, in industry directories, or from planning insiders, John should have contacted a community business group or requested information from the company's personnel or public relations manager. If all else failed, he should have reserved his barrage of questions for his informational interview with Jane Doe. Finally, John imposes his own schedule on Jane Doe, requesting that they meet during a certain time frame and that she call him to arrange the meeting. While he means to demonstrate his eager enthusiasm, John Smith's lack of preparation, poorly crafted and error-ridden letter, and presumptuous tone will only serve to insult and alienate his prospective contact.

Now consider the following letter, written by fictitious high school senior Mary Brown to regional planner John Doe.

Mary Brown
100 Main Street
Metropolis, State 10010

February 1, 2003

John Doe
ABC Planning
300 Front Street
Metropolis, State 10010

Dear Mr. Doe:

I am writing to request information about internships and volunteer opportunities at ABC Planning. Susan Ward of the Metropolis Historical Society suggested I contact you. I am eager to expand my knowledge and understanding of the issues facing urban planners today, and I feel that ABC's small staff and research-oriented mission would provide the ideal environment for my pre-professional development.

I will graduate from Metropolis Central High School in May. In fall 2003, I will begin my freshman year at State University, where I plan to major in architecture and take a broad selection of courses in environmental studies, political science, and community development. My class work and extracurricular experience have provided me with a solid introduction to economics, art history, and data analysis. As an active member in the Metropolis Youth Community Development League, I have firsthand experience in surveying sites and conducting extensive demographic research. I have also completed the State University Architecture Institute's Summer Youth Program, a six-week program for high school students committed to the study of urban design.

91

I would appreciate the opportunity to speak with you at your convenience and observe your work environment first-hand. I can be reached at the above address or by phone at 222-6666.

Thank you for your time.

Sincerely,
Mary Brown

Mary's letter states her request immediately, making her aim clear and concise. She successfully conveys her enthusiasm while presenting her relevant experiences and skills in a straightforward, crisp, professional manner. She also makes reference to ABC's particular planning style, structure, and office environment, and politely requests an informational interview. Furthermore, she implicitly includes a character reference by mentioning historical society employee Susan Ward.

Throughout, Mary's tone is professional, yet friendly. She is polite, yet assertive. She is respectful of John Doe's schedule, but she does not underestimate her own qualifications. Finally, her letter is free from the commonplace clichés and spelling errors that undermined the enthusiasm of John Smith's letter. When working on a word processor, always take advantage of the spell check function and reread your letter to check for grammatical errors and misused words. Don't hesitate to take your letter to a teacher, guidance counselor, or writing center volunteer to have a second set of eyes look at it, catch mistakes, and make suggestions for improvement. A letter of introduction makes an important first impression and will probably determine whether or not you get called in for an interview.

Between two and three weeks after sending her letter, Mary might consider following up with a brief, pleasant phone call to John Doe. It is important to remember, though, that many professionals, including urban planners, have extremely busy schedules driven by pressing deadlines. In any job search, it is important to be persistent but respectful.

Networking from the Inside

Working as an intern or volunteer at a public, private, or nonprofit firm will provide you with the opportunity to test your sustained interest in the field, increase your knowledge, and strengthen your résumé. You may find yourself working in a company or organization with a well-developed program in which interns and volunteers are supervised and mentored by experienced planners. This kind of program can provide the structure needed for an intensive, systematic learning experience.

If you find yourself in an internship or volunteer post without this structure, however, do no despair. This will be a test of your own determination, enthusiasm, and initiative, and you must confidently rise to the challenge. Make an effort to talk to all of the employees, asking them about their educational backgrounds, the path they took to get here, their own roles in the planning process, and what advice they might offer a future planner. Over lunch, at the water cooler, or during the company softball game, try to find out as much about their professional development as you can without appearing nosy. What attracted them to planning? How had their education prepared them for their real world experiences, if at all? In what ways were they unprepared for the job that lay ahead of them? What aspects of their job do they find particularly enjoyable? What parts of the job are difficult? What do they consider their professional strengths? What about their weaknesses? How do their previous jobs in planning compare to their current employment? What is the next career step for them? What will the next position or job title involve? Do they plan to make career changes in the future? How will these new endeavors build on their experience in planning? What should you, as a young person interested in planning, do to better prepare yourself for each stage of your career?

Make it known to your supervisor that you are eager to learn and enthusiastic about taking on new and varied responsibilities. You may not think you want to be an accountant, but be sure to spend some time with the organization's financial analysts. All planning projects are dependent on the financial resources available, and the budget can be a powerful tool or a frustrating limitation. It is important for a successful planner to understand the economics of development. A planner who consistently brings projects in over budget or badly underestimates projected costs is not likely to last long in the job (if she or he works for a firm or agency) or get much repeat business (if she or he runs the firm). For similar reasons, you should familiarize yourself with the legal, design, environmental, and public health issues associated with the firm's projects. These are planning areas that you will most likely have to address almost every day once you become a working planner. No successful project can be designed, pitched, and realized without careful attention to them.

So take advantage of the fact that you have not yet committed to specializing in any one aspect of urban planning or community development. Experiment and explore while you have the freedom to do so!

For Your Community

Teens are playing an increasingly important role in urban planning. Public policy makers, planners, architects, and parents express a growing concern for the development of safe, positive teen spaces—public meeting places such as recreation centers where young people can meet and enjoy themselves without fear for their safety. These adults are increasingly turning to teens themselves to help find answers to the tough questions: How do we get teens involved in our project? What makes a teen space "cool," while also safe and financially viable? How do we attract teens to established community environments? How do we create new environments especially for teens? Community-wide teen curfews, the construction of public skate parks, and the formation of social action groups targeting teen-specific issues are three very distinct ways of providing both opportunities and restrictions that aim to solve some of the social problems facing young people today.

Teens, however, are also taking an active role independent of adults in rejuvenating and maintaining positive community environments. Teens are founding and participating in a variety of community development programs ranging from conservation corps (which seek to refurbish and maintain neighborhoods) to community art projects, from opening their own businesses to organizing community bike rides and charitable fund-raising. Though distinct in focus, all of these activities are essentially acts of community planning and development.

The following real-life organizations are made possible by the efforts of children and young adults who want to make a difference in their communities while also having fun and gaining valuable planning experience to put on their résumé. This list provides just a glimpse of some of the hundreds of community organizations eager for your enthusiasm, energy, and experience. Information about these and other groups can be found on the Internet, at your local library, museum, historical society, community center, high school or college, or by word of mouth. Ask your guidance counselor and teachers how to get involved. Flip through the phone book, and request a packet of informational materials from organizations that interest you. There are countless ways to get involved right now!

Chain Reaction, Washington, D.C.

Chain Reaction was founded by members of the EcoDesign Corps, a program sponsored by Shaw EcoVillage, a Washington, D.C.–based nonprofit organization committed to encouraging young adult leaders and building successful communities. Shaw EcoVillage provides technical training, internships and employment, and mentoring programs for young people. The EcoDesign Corps conducted a study of Washington's transportation system, agricultural lands, and urban green spaces. The students concluded that, while bicycles are the most cost-effective, environmentally-sound vehicles on the road and provide numerous health and personal safety benefits, they are the least-used form of transportation in Washington, D.C., with ridership lagging far behind private automobiles and public transit. To boost bicycle popularity, the students recommended the creation of a bicycle recycling program. The program, named Chain Reaction, opened its doors for business on May 5, 2001.

Chain Reaction was organized to encourage the development of physical, financial, entrepreneurial, and interpersonal skills among young people between the ages of eleven and nineteen. To become a member, young adults are required to take a three-hour class in bicycle safety. After completing the course, they are eligible to participate in a variety of bicycle-related activities scheduled after school and on weekends. The group sponsors bike rides to historic sites and areas of natural beauty, including Roosevelt Park, Fort Dupont, and the National Mall. The annual Bike Rodeo provides a showcase for riders skilled in tricks and for demonstrations of bike safety. Experienced members are encouraged to join the Urban Racers, a junior racing team.

Most important, the organization opened a storefront business in which several young adults, trained by volunteer mechanics and supervised by an adult program manager, repair and resuscitate donated bicycles that are then sold to provide financial support for the program. In the first year alone, Chain Reaction mechanics repaired more than 500 bicycles and restored sixty donated bicycles. In addition, members can enroll in classes in bicycle mechanics, bike safety, and the role of bikes in the community. In so doing, they earn points, known as shop dollars, that are put toward acquiring a recycled bicycle.

Chain Reaction has had a significant effect on the community it serves and the students who participate in its bicycle-friendly activities. The storefront is located near a local elementary school and a junior high school, but the area is congested with traffic and not welcoming to young people. Vacant lots and the lack of shops and businesses made the area a haven for loiterers and drug dealers. The establishment of Chain Reaction has done much to revitalize the neighborhood and welcome young people to the area. In addition, it provides a worthwhile, goal-oriented activity for young adults. In 2001, one hundred students joined the organization, and 150 local residents attended the Bike Rodeo. These young adults established a community of fellow enthusiasts and learned valuable skills in the process. Chain Reaction is a successful community development organization conceived and maintained by hardworking young people committed to both community improvement and self-improvement.

Community YouthMapping, Denver, Colorado

The Denver, Colorado, YouthMapping program is one of more than thirty such programs across the country. The program is the brainchild of the Center for Youth Development and Policy Research (CYDPR) and is sponsored locally by the Piton Foundation. The CYDPR was created in 1990 to study and prepare youngsters for the issues facing American youth.

One of the organization's primary goals is to make more people, opportunities, and public spaces available for teens. Participants in the Community YouthMapping program became small-scale ethnographers in their own communities. They mapped their cities block-by-block, identifying both areas that are teen-friendly and areas that are in need of different kinds of teen-oriented spaces. In so doing, they became familiar with the tools of planning and community development and gained a new understanding of the way their cities are laid out and where opportunities for youth development are available. Many were even inspired to become more involved with their community's development.

The Denver public school system was anxious to get its students involved in community activities after school. To research and organize this effort, the school system enlisted the aid of the Piton Foundation and recruited students through the city's social service system, depending in part on the juvenile justice department. In other communities, students were enlisted through peer leadership programs, school organizations, and word of mouth. Students were paid for their involvement and for the opportunity to exercise their analytical and communication skills. The student researchers had to complete a training program to learn how to create and conduct surveys and process research data. Armed with questionnaires, the students took to the streets to discover what resources were available to teens through local nonprofit organizations, churches, businesses, youth groups, and schools. The teenagers went door-to-door, neighborhood-by-neighborhood—a painstaking job that required dedication and hard work.

In addition to giving the participants a sense of community and training them to be adept in several valuable skills, the YouthMapping program created a body of information about the youth of America and the social services available to them.This data bank can be utilized by community developers, politicians, and nonprofit organizations eager to address the concerns of young adults. Most important, this information is collected and processed by young adults, who offer a unique perspective on the research that adults cannot provide.

Prospect Park Youth Council, Brooklyn, New York

In the early 1860s, the borough of Brooklyn undertook its most expensive and remarkable public endeavor to date: Prospect Park. Landscape designers Frederick Law Olmsted and Calvert Vaux (the designers of New York's Central Park, the National Zoo in Washington, D.C., the sprawling Fairmount Park in Philadelphia, and Boston's Emerald Necklace) were commissioned to build a 526-acre natural haven in the middle of Brooklyn's rapidly growing urban community. They created a sixty-acre lake and a ninety-acre meadow, while preserving Brooklyn's last natural forest, which runs along the center of the park. Though the park would confront issues of safety and hard financial times throughout its history, today it is the jewel of Brooklyn envisioned by its earliest proponents. It receives a steady stream of local visitors and out-of-town tourists. Concerts, historical reenactments, and impromptu family picnics create a lively buzz of activity at Prospect Park all year round. The park, whose gently rolling hills were sculpted, in part, by glacial activity at the end of the last ice age, is also home to solitude seekers, outdoor yoga classes, and strolling couples of all ages. Though one of New York's greatest public gathering places, it can also offer a rare escape from the city's bustling crowds.

In 1998, the Prospect Park Alliance (PPA), a non-profit organization that maintains the park and organizes its program of activities, realized that young adults were not represented by the governing bodies of the various park departments. Furthermore, the calendar of PPA-sponsored activities, geared toward the young families that live in the surrounding neighborhoods, lacked teen-oriented events. To address this issue, the PPA formed the Youth Council.

The Youth Council is a group of committed young people between the ages of fourteen and twenty-one. New members are recruited by existing members, who sign up fellow students, present informational meetings for local groups, and make dozens of phone calls to teens who express interest. In the end, they generally enlist thirty-five to forty-five members each year, and the group usually slims down to twenty core members who take advantage of the leadership opportunities available to them.

The Youth Council is instrumental in several major park events each year. Council members organize the Teen Summit in conjunction with the Brooklyn Public Library, an event geared toward attracting young people to the library. The Youth Council is also responsible for talent shows, dog shows, evenings of swing dance, hip-hop parties, and teen-oriented celebrations of Earth Day. Council members take classes on leadership, park

101

history and maintenance, and community outreach. The members travel to Albany, the state capital, each year to lobby for park department issues before the state congress. They undertake community development research by sending out questionnaires and conducting phone surveys. They contribute to park maintenance by participating in preservation projects and working as youth guides. They also experience the administrative side of park life, orchestrating the volunteer efforts of outside organizations and community outreach groups. In addition, they staff the PPA's cottage, where young people can come to hang out, get help with their homework, or research employment opportunities within the parks department.

Members of the Prospect Park Youth Council feel genuinely influential and involved in their community. The PPA gives the Youth Council the authority to take initiative and make real contributions at Prospect Park, and the teen members rise to this challenge.

The Bardstown Road Youth Cultural Center, Louisville, Kentucky

In 1996, a group of civic-minded Louisville, Kentucky, teens joined together and conceived of a teen-oriented community center. They researched grant opportunities and hunted for available spaces. Two years later, the city offered the group a substantial grant to get started, and in April 2000, the doors to the Bardstown Road Youth Cultural Center, also known as the BRYCC (pronounced "brick") House, opened.

The 14,000-square-foot center occupies an entire floor of a former movie theater on Bardstown Road, and there are plans to expand onto another floor. Their mission, to promote creative expression, independent development, community consciousness, and youth activism, is achieved through a variety of programs run by semi-independent cooperatives (an organization owned and operated by those who benefit from its services). The Radio Collective broadcasts youth DJs. The Noise Collective organizes all BRYCC House musical events. The Art Collective presents art exhibits and promotes artists who work outside of the mainstream art scene. A library and computer lab provide a place for teens to do homework or read independently-published books for young people. At the former theater's concession stand, snacks and soda are for sale. A monthly poetry slam (a poetry reading contest), held in cooperation with the Louisville Poets' Guild, awards cash prizes to its winning participants. Social action groups use the space to hold meetings.

BRYCC House is overseen by a board of directors. According to the bylaws of the center's original charter, at least half of the board members must be young adults between the ages of thirteen and twenty-four. The other members are adults who have experience in fundraising, teen and community development, or nonprofit organization. The center prides itself on being youth-run and on maintaining a "non-hierarchical" philosophy toward its development and structure, meaning that there are no levels of power or rank within the group. Every active volunteer is given a vote when the center's assembly meets to decide questions of programming and administrative organization.

The center is praised in the local press for creating an underground music scene that rivals that supported by professional, experienced music promoters. Many of the center's initial goals, including broadcasting the BRYCC radio station over the Internet, have been achieved, and new volunteers continue to join. The center is seen as one of the brightest spots on Bardstown Road. The owners of the building in which it is housed believe the center keeps the neighborhood safe, clean, and positive. It is concrete proof that a well-designed civic center can bring about a strong sense of community, productivity, and purpose to a neighborhood.

Breaking New Ground

If you have thoroughly researched the youth organizations operating in your area, and you find that they do not fulfill their mission or do not appeal to your

World Town Planning Day

Sponsored by the American Institute of Certified Planners (AICP), World Town Planning Day (November 8) celebrates the contributions of community and regional planning to the quality of life of human settlements and their environment. It is designed to promote awareness, support, and advocacy of community and regional planning among the general public and politicians in all levels of government. It is celebrated in thirty countries on four continents.

interests, consider starting one of your own. Start
small, and gradually build on your successes. You do
not want an enterprise to fail because you took on too
much too quickly. Though youth organizations discussed in this chapter might offer inspiration to get
involved, they do not represent a standard against
which your own efforts should be judged. Keep in
mind that the young adults who conceived of, organized, and maintained these organizations did so with
the help of their peers and adults. Their efforts took
time, money, determination, and skill. As you approach
any project, set reasonable, but challenging, goals for
yourself. Ask for assistance, and eagerly accept all the
help you can get. Be willing to recognize your mistakes, learn from them, and move on, while still
remaining true to your overall vision.

If you have decided to address a problem that you
have identified in your neighborhood, follow the following steps. First, study your community carefully. If
there are few or unsuccessful youth organizations
operating in the area, ask yourself why this is. What is
it about your community or these organizations that
discourages young people from getting involved? In
what areas do you see the need for community
activism? Are your neighborhood parks littered with
garbage? Does graffiti decorate your school or other
public buildings? Is there a comprehensive recycling
program in place at your school? Do teens in your area
have an organized public meeting place, such as a
skate park, a youth garden, or a studio to work on
visual art projects? Do others share your opinion concerning what the youth of the community need? Talk
to friends and family members about what they think

is in need of improvement. Research past community efforts in archived newspaper and magazine articles at your local library or on the Internet. Talk to teachers, your postal worker, a police officer, or a crossing guard to get a broad cross section of opinions from people intimately familiar with the daily workings of your neighborhood. When you have identified a problem, consider the possible solutions and ask these same people which, if any, they think is the most appropriate. Refer to books and Web sites that chronicle the successes and failures of past community development projects elsewhere in the country. Learn from their experiences and consider how to apply this new understanding to your own situation. Use your imagination, too. You may devise a successful solution that no one has ever thought of and has never been tried before!

Responding to the needs of a community is a complicated endeavor, and when you have decided on several possible courses of action, you should begin by approaching an adult who can serve as an adviser and representative. The adviser can use his or her experience and influence to both highlight weaknesses in your plan, sharpen its focus, and help gather support for it out in the community. Like all planning projects, yours will rely heavily on creativity and experimentation to create a program of activities that meets the needs of your community. Communities are not built or improved overnight. Both volunteer and professional urban planning requires a great deal of patience and understanding. But the results can be remarkable, as we have just seen.

The Future of Urban Planning

The future of urban planning—and our cities—may hinge upon the outcome of a philosophical battle that has been raging in the planning field for several decades. It concerns diametrically opposed visions of what a city should look like, how it should be organized, and how it should function. Will future cities return to earlier models of urban life—featuring multicultural neighborhoods that contain homes, businesses, parks, and administrative offices? Or will they begin to follow a more suburban model of sprawl, cultural homogeneity, and separated zones of commerce, residences, public spaces, and municipal buildings?

Jacobs's Great City

In her groundbreaking 1961 book, *The Death and Life of Great American Cities*, Jane Jacobs proposed that the life of a city is like a ballet and that this ballet is played out on many public stages—the sidewalk, the park, the subway station, the courtyard, the library, the museum, and the civic center, to name a few. Some of these public spaces are successful, and some of them are not, and this, Jacobs argues, depends on several factors.

A successful sidewalk, Jacobs says, is one on which there is a balance of public and private life. It should feature distinct and widely accessible public spaces (such as shops and cafes) that keep people busy, and well-defined private spaces (such as fountain gardens), to which one can retreat in solitude. Jacobs believes a successful sidewalk must attract a group of "regulars," whether they are children at play, loiterers, adults rushing from place to place running errands, or store owners standing idly on their front stoops. Finally, a successful sidewalk is one with eyes, where every resident, shopkeeper, and passerby has an unconscious sense of obligation to protect everyone else and the structures surrounding them. These theories can be applied to all neighborhoods, regardless of their socioeconomic status.

At the time, Jacobs's theories were largely rejected as violating every thing contemporary urban planning theory believed to be true. Prior to the 1960s, planners advocated urban renewal plans derived from the Garden City theories of more than half a century before. The products of their labors, notably many of New York's massive subsidized housing projects, combined the courtyard design of the Garden City with the skyscraper height of the modern cityscape. In so doing, Jacobs argued, these communities blurred the line between public and private space. Residents either remained in their apartments or congregated in interior courtyards while the streets and sidewalks beyond the housing complexes became empty of strollers and shoppers, and were instead often given over to crime.

Jacobs's theories were largely the product of observation and personal research. She was not a practicing planner with a degree in architecture, urban design, or community development. She did not graduate from college. Instead, she spent hours watching the movement of people through public parks, she spoke to professional planners and compared their opinions with her own observations, and she spoke to county social workers, business owners, and passersby on the street. Most important, she spoke to people who lived in underdeveloped or poorly developed neighborhoods, people who lived near parks they were afraid to enter after dark, and people who didn't let their children play in the courtyards and public balconies of the projects in which they lived.

Perhaps more than any other professional endeavor, the planning process aims to incorporate the desires and opinions of entire communities. While a medical doctor may diagnose a condition, explain methods of treatment, prescribe a cure, and perform a procedure, the urban planner depends heavily on the input of the "patient," or city dweller. This is because, as Jacobs argues, urban planning is not an exact science. While there may be general principles and solutions that have worked somewhere else at some other time, the process of solving urban problems requires close study of the particular situation at a given area and creative solutions.

Today, Jacobs's theories are widely taught in planning schools and frequently practiced by professional planning organizations. They still do not enjoy universal acceptance, however.

The Decentered City

Another significant work of late-twentieth century urban theory is Christopher Alexander, Sara Ishikawa, and Murrary Silverstein's *A Pattern Language*, the third volume in a series published in the late 1970s. This book is also well regarded by many architects and planners, but it presents a distinct perspective on urban planning, one that differs markedly from Jane Jacob's ideas.

The authors assert that urban planning and architectural design are a science to the same extent that language is a science. There is a body of possible urban patterns—in *A Pattern Language*, the authors present 253 such patterns—that work like the words of a sentence or, with increasing scope, a paragraph or a book. *A Pattern Language* is organized in short chapters, and each chapter outlines a different pattern. For example, chapter 8 describes a pattern called Mosaic of Subcultures, which asserts that the homogeneous nature of modern cities stifles the variety of lifestyles of its residents and impedes personal development. Consequently, cities should be divided into distinct areas where subcultures—not economically or ethnically segregated neighborhoods—can exist on their own and are given the space to thrive as semi-independent units. In subsequent chapters, the authors argue that cities themselves are prisons, and humans need access to the countryside to revive their spirits.

In each chapter, a pattern is defined, evidence is given for its validity, and a solution is proposed to promote positive community development. The patterns can be chosen and combined in any number of variations to create flexible plans ranging in scope from a single residence to an entire region with a population of several million.

Like any language, these patterns exist spontaneously. They develop organically, as a series of chance accidents and random actions—they are not as effective when achieved through government regulation. And, like any language, the patterns themselves are evolving all the time through human contact and usage. A development that is appropriate in one community context is not in another, just as slang is an inappropriate form of language during a job interview. A development project that made sense thirty years ago may no longer work in a twenty-first-century urban context, just as Shakespearian English is no longer useful to us in everyday conversation.

As suggested by these examples, *A Pattern Language* promotes a largely decentralized philosophy, arguing that large cities are economically and ecologically oppressive and unworkable. Metropolitan areas should be broken up into politically and culturally independent regions. The population should be divided into many small towns and even smaller farms. People should come together in public spaces, such as beer halls, bus stations, and pedestrian streets, but the home and other private buildings—made up of a series of smaller buildings and never more than four stories tall—would be separate and distinct from the city's public spaces. In effect, residential areas would be smaller, set-apart clusters within the web of the city.

The Cities of Tomorrow

A Pattern Language presents a theory of urban planning that, like that proposed in Jacobs's *The Death and Life of Great American Cities*, is the product of research and observation. However, the two books differ in vastly important ways. By considering them together, we see one of the central conflicts of urban planning theory of the past sixty years, one that has not yet been resolved. Jacobs celebrates the traditional city and urges a return to its harmonious mix—city block by city block—of public spaces, private dwellings, commercial activity, and multicultural expression. The authors of *A Pattern Language* instead proclaim the death of the traditional city. In its place, they argue, should rise a connected series of smaller, culturally distinct towns within the city, which share certain public and commercial spaces.

Within this philosophical clash lies the likely future of urban planning in the twenty-first century. Will our cities return to a more neighborhood-based model, in which residents can shop, stroll, dine, and seek entertainment within a few blocks of their home? Will this strong sense of community result in a lessening of suburbanization, as individuals and families return to renewed and civilized urban life? Or will suburbanization continue to draw away city residents and create a sprawling metropolis where the point at which the city ends and the suburbs begin is increasingly hazy? Will the city center shatter outward creating a scattered collection of distinct and separate regions that will more resemble a sort of urban suburb? The answers to these questions reside in economic, demographic, political, and cultural forces that are not entirely predictable. They also rely, however, on the vision and ideals of future planners like you.

Urban planning combines the lessons of yesterday and the experiments of tomorrow. Driven by cities, which are the bastions of history and the centers of the modern age, urban planners must always consider the past and the future. Think again of the city street, park, museum, or other public space discussed in the first chapter of this book. Can you trace the history of the neighborhood's development in its buildings and public spaces? Can you identify any concerns neighborhood residents or visitors might have about the area? Who would you talk to if you wanted to find out more about an issue? Can you think of ways that you could benefit the community? If this sort of activity excites you, consider a career in urban planning—our cities and towns need your enthusiasm!

Glossary

advocacy The process of supporting a plan, group, or individual.

aesthetics A branch of philosophy dealing with the nature of beauty, art, and taste.

blight The deterioration of urban areas.

canal A human-made inland waterway.

canvass To conduct a survey of public opinion; to poll.

City Beautiful An urban design movement that was characterized by monumental public buildings and spaces.

commercial Relating to business and commerce.

Community Development Block Grants (CDBG) Government aid provided for community development plans.

Community Development Corporation (CDC) A nonprofit
  partnership between community-based social
  activists and local businesses.
consultants People who give professional advice
  to others.
Council on Environmental Quality (CEQ) A federal review
  agency created by the National Environmental
  Policy Act.
decentralization Moving the majority of residential,
  commercial, or political power outside of the
  center of a city or the capital of a state or country.
demographic Relating to the characteristic of the
  people of an area.
Department of Housing and Urban Development (HUD)
  The federal agency that proposes, implements, and
  reviews government urban plans.
Environmental Protection Agency (EPA) A federal agency
  that reviews and regulates the actions and plans of
  all federal agencies.
federal Relating to the central government of the
  country.
freelance Not employed by an organization; self-
  employed person who provides work for another
  person or company for a fee.
Garden City A theoretical rural town that would
  incorporate large commonly-held green spaces
  into residential and business areas.
Great Depression A period of serious economic
  decline during the late 1920s and 1930s.
hierarchy The division of people into increasingly
  important positions of authority.

high occupancy vehicle (HOV) An automobile that contains one or more passengers in addition to the driver.

infrastructure The basic framework of a city, including its buildings, bridges, tunnels, and public utilities.

lobby To try to influence public affairs through government officials.

low-income housing Affordable housing provided for people who earn less money.

manifest destiny The belief that motivated American expansion west toward the Pacific Ocean for the purposes of financial gain and religious missionary work.

maritime Relating to the sea.

municipal Relating to the affairs of a local government.

nonprofit Not for the purpose of making money; these organizations are given special status by the government that reduces their taxation.

ordinances Laws established by a governmental body.

permits Official documents stating permission to do something.

precedent An earlier legal case that was argued and decided on similar grounds.

public utilities Services, including water, gas, and heat, provided by local governments.

quota A limited share.

residential Used as a home.

seminar A group of advanced students gathered together to share their research.

single occupancy vehicle (SOV) An automobile that contains only the driver.

subdivisions Tracts of land divided into plots, developed upon, and sold.

subsidize To offer financial assistance from one person or government to another; partial financial support from public funds.

suburbanization The mass movement of city dwellers to the suburbs and the conversion of arable farmland into these residential areas.

suburban sprawl The expansion of low-lying buildings, parking lots, and roads in suburban areas.

suburbs The outlying areas of a city or town.

Tammany Hall The headquarters of the Tammany Society, a powerful political organization in New York during the late nineteenth century.

tenement An apartment house meeting the minimum standards of public health and safety.

Urban Development Action Grant (UDAG) Federal aid programs for urban development programs.

utopian Having to do with an ideal social organization and the perfectibility of human society.

zoning The division of land into areas regulated for specific kinds of development.

For More Information

American Planning Association
122 South Michigan Avenue, Suite 1600
Chicago, IL 60603
(312) 431-9100
Web site: http://www.planning.org

Canadian Centre for Architecture
1920 Baile Street,
Montréal, PQ Canada H3H 2S6
(514) 939-7026
Web site: http://cca.qc.ca

Canadian Council on Social Development
309 Cooper Street, 5th Floor
Ottawa, ON Canada K2P 0G5
(613) 236-8977
Web site: http://www.ccsd.ca

Canadian Institute of Planners
116 Albert Street, Suite 801
Ottawa, ON Canada K1P 5G3
(800) 207-2138

(613) 237-PLAN (7526)
Web site: http://www.cip-icu.ca

Canadian Urban Institute
100 Lombard Street, Suite 400
Toronto, ON Canada M5C 1M3
(416) 365-0816
Web site: http://www.canurb.com

Columbia University
Graduate School of Architecture, Planning,
    and Preservation
400 Avery Hall
New York, NY 10021
(212) 854-3510
Web site: http://www. arch.columbia.edu

Metropolitan Planning Council
25 East Washington Street, Suite 1600
Chicago, IL 60602
(312) 922-5616
Web site: http://www.metroplanning.org

National Building Museum
401 F Street NW
Washington, DC 20001
(202) 272-2448
Web site: http://www.nbm.org

The Octagon Museum
1799 New York Avenue NW
Washington, DC 20006
(202) 638-3221
Web site: http://www.archfoundation.org/octagon

University of Michigan
Taubman College of Architecture and Urban Planning
2000 Bonisteel Boulevard
Ann Arbor, MI 48109-2069
(734) 764-1300
Web site: http://www.tcaup.umich.edu

University of Wisconsin–Milwaukee
School Of Architecture and Urban Planning
P.O. Box 413
Milwaukee, WI 53201
(414) 229-4014
Web site: http://www.uwm.edu/SARUP

The Urban Institute
2100 M Street NW
Washington, DC 20037
(202) 833-7200
Web site: http://www.urban.org

Web Sites

Due to the changing nature of Internet links, the Rosen
Publishing Group, Inc., has developed an online list of
Web sites related to the subject of this book. This site is
updated regularly. Please use this link to access the list:

http://www.rosenlinks.com/crl/urpl/

For Further Reading

Books

Alexander, Christopher, et al., eds. *A Pattern Language: Towns, Buildings, Construction*. New York: Oxford University Press, 1977.

Alexander, Ernest R. *Approaches to Planning: Introducing Current Planning Theories, Concepts, and Issues*. Philadelphia, PA: Gordon and Breach, 1992.

Barnett, Jonati. *An Introduction to Urban Design*. New York: Harper and Row, 1982.

Brophy, Paul C., and Alice Shabecoff. *A Guide to Careers in Community Development*. Washington, DC: Island Press, 2001.

Cohen, Nahoum. *Urban Planning, Conservation, and Preservation*. New York: McGraw-Hill, 2001.

Cullingworth, Barry. *Planning in the USA: Policies, Issues, and Processes*. London: Routledge, 1997.
Garreau, Joel. *Edge City: Life on the New Frontier*. New York: Doubleday, 1991.
Gelfand, Mark I. *A Nation of Cities: The Federal Government and Urban America*. New York: Oxford University Press, 1975.
Jacobs, Jane. *The Death and Life of Great American Cities*. New York: Vintage Books, 1992.
Miles, Malcolm, Tim Hall, and Iain Borden, eds. *The City Cultures Reader*. London: Routledge, 2000.
Stein, Jay M., ed. *Classic Readings in Urban Planning*. New York: McGraw-Hill, 1995.

Web Journals

Berkeley Planning Journal
http://www.dcrp.ced.berkeley.edu/bpj

The Brookings Institute
http://www.brookings.edu/urban

Carolina Planning Journal
http://www.unc.edu/depts/dcrpweb/carplan

Critical Planning
http://www.sppsr.ucla.edu/critplan

Innovative Urban Planning
http://www.columbia.edu/~jws150/urban_planning

Journal of the American Planning Association
http://www.japa.pdx.edu

The New Urban Agenda (Canada)
http://www.peck.ca/nua/nua.html

Planetizen
http://www.planetizen.com

The Planning Commissioners Journal
http://www.plannersweb.com

University College London's Care for Advanced Spatial
      Analysis, Online Planning (United Kingdom)
http://www.casa.ucl.ac.uk/online.htm

Index

About the Author

Gillian Houghton is an editor and freelance writer in New York City. As a newcomer to the city, she is fascinated by its complex interworkings and has a newfound appreciation for the challenges of urban planning.

Series Design

Danielle Goldblatt

Layout

Tahara Hasan

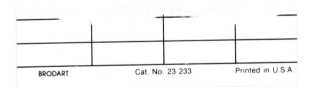